# way
# to go

# way to go

Thirty readings on a
journey with Jesus

## Eddie Gibbs
with meditations by Brian Draper

**ivp**

Inter-Varsity Press

INTER-VARSITY PRESS
*38 De Montfort Street, Leicester LE1 7GP, England*
*Email: ivp@uccf.org.uk*
*Website: www.ivpbooks.com*

*First published 2003*

**British Library Cataloguing in Publication Data**
A catalogue record for this book is available from the British Library.

ISBN 0–85111–286–2

Set in Rotis 9.5/13pt
Typeset in Great Britain by CRB Associates, Reepham, Norfolk
Printed and bound in Great Britain by Creative Print and Design (Wales), Ebbw
Vale

*Inter-Varsity Press is the publishing division of the Universities and Colleges
Christian Fellowship (formerly the Inter-Varsity Fellowship), a student
movement linking Christian Unions in universities and colleges throughout
Great Britain, and a member movement of the International Fellowship of
Evangelical Students. For more information about local and national activities
write to UCCF, 38 De Montfort Street, Leicester LE1 7GP, email us at
email@uccf.org.uk or visit the UCCF website at www.uccf.org.uk.*

# Contents

# Preparing for the journey

An encounter with Jesus is life-transforming

In the following pages we will meet people whose encounter with Jesus turned their lives upside-down. They were never the same again. Through him they discovered such a profound faith in God that they had to share it with others. For some the encounter was unsought. For others it was the fulfilment of a lifetime's search or the meeting of an urgent personal need. They were people from all walks of life, from the pillars of society to the gutters. They were religious and irreligious, male and female, Jew and Gentile.

Nobody loves quite like Jesus or sees so deeply and clearly into the soul of people. In Part 1 we will learn from his example as we read about how he dealt with an extraordinary collection of individuals. His approach is flexible, diverse and just right for the person concerned. Often we will eavesdrop on the rich dialogue that takes place. With no hint of coercion or a sales pitch, Jesus always recognizes and honours the dignity and uniqueness of other people.

In Part 2 we will travel in company with Jesus and his disciples. We will find our lives changing as we walk alongside him and the others who are learning lessons along the way. We will spend six days pouring over the central teachings of Jesus found in the Sermon on the Mount. We will learn what companionship with him entails and what impact it will have on every area of our life.

In Part 3 we will conclude with three significant events recorded in Acts in which Peter, Philip and Paul share the liberating message of Jesus. They, like us, struggled with their human limitations in trying to meet people at their point of need.

### Before starting

Some books you can skim read in a few hours at one sitting. This book is different. Read a section at a time, one day at a time. For each day, there is a Bible passage to look up. Please read it through slowly at least three times. Then turn to the meditation provided to further stimulate your thinking. It is intended as a prompter not as an exhaustive commentary on the passage. So, if your thinking takes you in a different direction from the recorded points, that's OK. If you find that you need more than one day to think through and apply a chapter, that's fine too. Then there's a question or something to ponder on for each day, and a poem to read, which takes another look at the theme of the chapter.

Don't hurry your reading, for these daily meditations are designed to lead to daily action. But do not be bound by the resolutions suggested here. The inner voice of God's Spirit may be prompting you to take a different course of action in response to your reading and meditation. The important thing is to learn to listen obediently to God, especially in his desire to touch other lives in simple yet profound ways. We need the expectancy and alertness to believe that those whose lives we touch God can transform.

One further suggestion: you might want to undertake this thirty-day journey in company with a small group of friends who are also followers of Jesus Christ. As we will see during the course of the next few days, witness is not simply one voice crying in the wilderness, but more often is the choral statement of the community of people of faith. If *Way to go* is used in a group context you may want to take one chapter a week rather than one a day.

My prayer is that these spiritual exercises will turn us all into more enthusiastic, credible and contagious Christ-followers. In his company we will constantly come across people who are not there by happenstance, but by divine appointment.

Eddie Gibbs
Pasadena, California, USA

# way
# to go

part 1

Beginning the
journey of a
lifetime

# day 1

# God makes the first move

Luke 2:8-20; Matthew 2:1-12

> 'The shepherds said, "Let's go to Bethlehem and see this thing that has happened."'
> 'Scholars from the east came to Jerusalem and asked, "Where is the one who has been born king of the Jews? We saw his star in the east and have come to worship him."'*

It was the most significant announcement ever to be made to this planet, namely the birth of the Son of God for the salvation of humankind. God had been preparing for this moment from before the foundation of the world. We must begin by appreciating this grand perspective.

God had prepared a specific group of people to welcome his Anointed One. He was, in the first place, the Saviour of Israel and then of the whole world. The Scriptures bore ample testimony to his promised coming, and day after day the Jewish scholars pored over the sacred texts. It therefore comes as a great surprise that the first public announcement of that event was not made to the priests and scholars in the Jerusalem temple, but to the humble shepherds on a Bethlehem hillside.

### The shepherds

Shepherds had an honourable place in the history of Israel. Just consider the patriarchs Jacob and Joseph, Moses, the leader of the nation, and David, her most famous king. But recently the reputation of shepherds had become tarnished to the point where they were generally considered as an untrustworthy class of people, rootless individuals who were here today and gone tomorrow. It was to such a group that God chose to make Mary's birth announcement.

Some people feel that they are too insignificant or that their reputation is too messed up for God to be bothered with them. They view religion as for the pundits and the reputable. But the Bible challenges such misguided assumptions. Time and time again God speaks to the most unlikely people and chooses a moment when they least expect it. In our story an angel makes the announcement to the sound of a massed choir of angels bursting into their chorus of praise to God. God seldom puts on such a spectacular show to reveal his purposes. But the spectacle was appropriate to the occasion. The shepherds were understandably terrified, but their fear was soon turned into irrepressible joy.

I suppose that the angelic announcer and the back-up choir could have repeated the performance, even gone on tour! But that was not God's way. The curtains of heaven are drawn back a fraction, and only for a few moments, to announce that, *'Today in the town of David a Saviour has been born to you; he is Christ the Lord.'* It is left to the shepherds to make the next move. They have to discover for themselves the truth of what the angel has declared. On finding Mary, Joseph and the baby, they immediately spread the word of what the angels had announced and how they had found it to be true. They were like journalists with the thrill of a scoop on today's front-page news story. The significant difference was that their announcement would be forever new to those who heard it for the first time.

The shepherds not only witnessed, they worshipped – two activities that belong together and reinforce each other. Their unique experience did not lead them to neglect their mundane responsibilities. They still had sheep to care for.

### The scholars

If the respectable in Israel looked down on shepherds, the theologians denounced the astrologers. Indeed, their clairvoyant arts are condemned in a number of places in the Old Testament and the Jews were strongly rebuked for consulting them. They should have known better, because they had a surer guide in the law God had revealed to them through Moses and the prophets. Yet God was more accommodating with the people of Babylon, who knew no better. More than that, he revealed himself to the most revered scholars of the day, astrologers, who sought significant portents from the movement of the planets.

The astrologers witnessed a strange astronomical phenomenon, the precise nature of which has been argued over for centuries. Was the bright star caused by the conjunction of the convergence of Jupiter and Saturn that occurred in 7–6 BC, or was it the appearance of a comet or the exploding of a supernova? We will probably never know, and its only importance is in the dating of the birth of Christ. At any rate, their investigations led them to the conclusion that this sign in the sky announced that the

Who are the shepherds and astrologers of our time? Pray for any you meet today.

Messiah-King had been born to the Jews. Who supplied them with this clue to its significance? The most likely explanation is that they learned it from the Jewish community which was still in Babylonia centuries after the bulk had returned from their Babylonian exile.

The intensity of their interest is shown by their willingness to make a long journey to find the newborn child. They even brought with them costly gifts worthy of a king. Naturally they go to Jerusalem first, the holy city of the Jews, to confer with the religious leaders to discover the birthplace of the Messiah.

Their joyful eagerness stands in stark contrast to the suspicion and unease of King Herod, who considered their questions to be so politically explosive that he became personally involved. In response to their request, he feigns cooperation by consulting with his religious advisors and giving their consensus. The location of the birth predicted by the prophets in the Scriptures was Bethlehem; he then arranged a secret meeting with the scholars to instruct them where to search and to make a private arrangement for them to return once they had found the baby. His intention was not to follow their example in worshipping the infant king, but to ensure the baby's death before the news got out and he became the centre of a popular uprising.

The contrast between the response of the Jewish king and his advisors and the scholars from the east could not be more stark. King Herod began to plot Jesus' death and his advisors showed no further interest, whereas the astrologers travelled many miles to find the baby and worship him. Today religious sociologists report a widespread spiritual search throughout the Western world. But unlike the scholars of the birth story of Jesus, today's seekers do not know where to look, and are often put off from looking by the very people who describe themselves as Christians.

God colours outside of the box. His initiatives are creative, unconventional and unexpected. But we often miss what he is actually doing due to our assumptions and prejudice. Today's stories alert us to the fact that God is working among the most unlikely people and in the most unexpected places. By his loving generosity he is reaching down through the layers of society to those who are the most despised – as well as up to those whom we consider, or who

**Have you ever been surprised by God? How can we be ready to hear his voice and respond?**

consider themselves, to be out of reach. He is also working with people who, from our vantage point, seem far away geographically or culturally. God has both a great heart and incredibly long and powerful arms – sufficient to reach out to you and me, and to those whom we might otherwise be tempted to consider beyond redemption.

### Shepherd's Delight

It should have been a quiet night;
we had little to do but tend the sheep,
talk about the weather and wonder
what the deep blue skies above might hold.

One of my biggest complaints –
and they'll all tell you so – is that
Nothing special ever happens to me.
But why should it? I'm nothing special.

Which makes that night so out of this world.

My wife tells me off for saying, 'It's only me!'
when I give a friend a call.
It's never only you, she says. I guess it takes
Someone else to really know.

I never used to believe her, but then –
they didn't just come to *only me*, did they?
It was simply divine; out of the blue.

Angel,
I think things are changing,
for good.

# day 2

# Come and see

John 1:35-42

> 'When John the Baptizer saw Jesus passing
> by, he said, "Look, the Lamb of God!"
> When his two followers heard John say this,
> they followed Jesus.'*

Our life-long journey of faith, as with any long-distance trek, proceeds by stages. Andrew and John began their spiritual journeys as followers of John the Baptizer. He was God's messenger crying in the wilderness. John was credible because of his authentic and passionate commitment to God. His surroundings, wardrobe and diet demonstrated that he wasn't in it for the money! He was also a man of courage, who didn't mince his words. He challenged injustice head-on and had zero tolerance for religious pretence. He demanded that his hearers should clean up their act, symbolized by a ritual washing in the Jordan river. Hence the name recorded in history, John the Baptizer.

The role of John the Baptizer was to announce the coming of the kingdom and to prepare God's people by his urgent appeals for repentance. He was not a preacher in the temple but a voice crying in the wilderness, a place of repentance and renewal. He baptized in the river Jordan, flowing along the frontier of the Promised Land. So when the baptized emerged from the water they represented another significant wave of occupation, just as it had been at the time of Joshua's conquest and, hundreds of years later, of the return from exile in Babylonia. The baptism of John gave notice that God was unfolding a new chapter in the history of his people.

In John's eyes established religion had lost all credibility. Consequently, he pointed people away from a corrupt institution toward the coming of God's reign, which he believed to be close at hand. Jesus, John the Baptizer's cousin, had journeyed from Galilee to be baptized by John as a way of showing his identification with sinful people. That significant event signalled the beginning of Jesus' ministry and the phasing out of John's. Soon after it, John pointed Jesus out to two of his closest followers declaring, *'Look, the Lamb of God!'*

Although this description may not communicate much today, it was an attention-getter as far as Peter and John were concerned. 'The Lamb of God' refers to the Passover lamb that they killed to commemorate God's anger passing over them, leaving them unharmed when God's judgment fell on Egypt for Pharaoh's refusal to release Israel from bondage. Animal sacrifice became central to the worship of Israel – it represented the transference of the guilt of their sins onto the substitute animal. The Feast of Passover, celebrated annually in the temple, was the most important pilgrimage of the year. The hills around Jerusalem were dotted with grazing flocks of sheep, ready for sacrifice in the temple. For Peter and John, a lamb dedicated to God represented an innocent one suffering on behalf of another. So from day one they knew that Jesus was destined to bear in his own person the sins of humankind.

John the Baptizer was no empire-builder. His concern was to prepare people to recognize and follow his Lord. When Jesus approached him in the midst of the crowd, John was not only reluctant to baptize Jesus; he confessed, *'I need to be baptised by you'* (Matthew 3:14). The task of the witness is always to point people to Jesus and not to attract a personal following. Likewise our goal must never be to gain control of a person's life but rather to influence them in order that God's purposes are fulfilled in their life.

There comes a moment with every human leader when it is time to say goodbye to them and move on. That individual has taken us as far as he or she is able. So now Peter and John leave John the Baptizer's company never to return. John the Baptizer had provided a half-way house for them. They now must follow the Lamb of God.

Jesus, realizing that he is being followed, turns to face them and asks, *'What do you want?'* Throughout his ministry Jesus was acutely aware when people took their first steps in following him, and what prompted them. He invites them to accompany him home and spend time with him. Little did they realize that this first encounter would represent a turning-point in their lives.

Any relationship takes time to develop and can deepen only on the basis of trust. Peter and John trusted John the Baptizer sufficiently to follow in the direction he now pointed. They had probably witnessed Jesus' baptism in the Jordan and were at least aware that John had singled him out in the crowd. They accepted his description of Jesus as 'the Lamb of God' by faith. It would be three more years before Jesus fulfilled the role that John saw with such prophetic clarity and certainty.

It was not the house they visited that day that was important: it was not Jesus' permanent address, but only his lodging place for the time that he was visiting Jerusalem. In the Gospels, Jesus is constantly on the move and we later learn that the Son of Man had nowhere to lay his head. But to be invited to someone's home often marks the real start of a relationship. And this was the beginning of a relationship that would change their lives.

However, Andrew and John immediately acknowledged that Jesus was their teacher – and that afternoon they received their first lesson, which lasted from 4 pm throughout the remainder of the day. We do not know what Jesus taught them on that visit. But one thing is clear – they came away convinced that Jesus was the one they should now be following.

We may define a witness as one individual who can tell another clearly and precisely how and where to find Jesus. But we cannot send people back to the place where *we* first found him. Rather we must accompany them to the place where we encounter Christ at this present time. In other words, our witness must be current, not a nostalgia trip. The invitation is always *'Come and see'*, never 'Go on your own to discover for yourself.'

Give thanks for where following Jesus has taken you in your life so far.

The relationship begun with Jesus that day could only be sustained if Peter and John were prepared to follow him wherever he went. But that is the subject for another day.

### Deep Water

It must be a thankless task
to be a voice crying in the wilderness,
to call others from where they're at
And to immerse them fully in another world.

It must be a lonely business
leading from the front,
often attracting the wrong kind of attention,
trying not to lose your head when all around you others are.

It must be a tough call
to give someone else the glory,
when so many try to give it back to you.
Where on earth can all this lead?

For a start, at least,
it leads me to you;
and you and I both
to Him.

## day 3

# Where to start

John 1:40-51

> 'The first thing Andrew did was to find his
> brother Simon ... Philip found Nathanael ...'

Most courses on sharing our faith and making known the good news of Jesus are really remedial classes. They are designed to help us overcome our personal inhibitions about speaking up for Christ and breaking the corporate silence maintained by God's community – and to unlearn our 'churchspeak', which is incomprehensible in the wider community.

Some of us also need to rekindle a faith that has grown cold with the passing of time. We may have to relearn the central purpose of the church, which is to live out its faith commitment in the world and to be able to answer the questions of people around us whose curiosity has been raised by our disturbingly different manner of life.

At the outset of Jesus' ministry we find two individuals who suffered no inhibitions in readily sharing the news that they had found the long-awaited Messiah. Andrew went to find his brother, Simon, and Philip his friend, Nathanael. They both acted promptly. In Andrew's case it was the first thing that he did. He acted spontaneously without any prompting, not to mention training! So Jesus returned to Galilee with a nucleus of followers accompanying him, three of whom, and probably all four, came from the town of Bethsaida located on the northern tip of the Sea of Galilee.

When Andrew brought his brother Simon to Jesus, he watched Jesus look him straight in the eye, with that penetrating gaze that pierced the soul. Then he heard him declare, *'You are Simon son of John. You will be called Cephas.'* This was an Aramaic name that translates into Greek as 'Peter' and means 'rock'. Andrew had lived with his brother's explosively unpredictable temperament. He was to see a rocket transformed into a rock. Peter was to provide that firm foundation on which a movement would be born after Jesus had left their earthly scene. From that very first day Jesus saw with prophetic clarity the role that Peter was destined to fulfil.

You and I, in contrast to Jesus, seldom know how widespread will be the influence of a single individual whom we have led to Christ. It is only years later, when we look back, that we are privileged to see how God has used that person, who perhaps did not seem so special to us at the time. We need the gift of discernment to see the God-given potential of those among whom we live and work, and to ensure that we become a catalyst and not an impediment to their achieving that potential.

Ask God to show you the potential of someone you have been sharing the gospel with or for whom you have been praying.

Once a person places his or her life into the hands of Jesus he can make a dramatic difference. Jesus accepts anyone without regard to his or her merits. He simply wants those who are teachable, even though they may be slow learners. But his unconditional love is not complacency. A *laissez-faire* attitude is not real love, in that it merely reinforces bad habits and destructive behaviour patterns. To be with Jesus brings about a profound transformation as we learn the kind of person he intends us to become and the purpose he has for our lives.

We see the same pattern repeated once again. Philip shares his discovery with his friend Nathanael. As with Andrew, the news about meeting Jesus is attractive to their whole circle of friends. This is the basis of witness. It is not arguing about ideas or promoting opinions. Only the argumentative and the opinionated are motivated to engage in those kinds of conversations. Meeting someone significant excites everyone, even the most shy and non-confrontational. Witness is also about telling as much as you know. There will always be more to share later, when you have discovered more, especially when you are learning together by being with Jesus.

Our effectiveness as witnesses is not in proportion to the number of years that we have been followers of Jesus Christ. In fact, it is often the new believer who makes the greatest impact. This is in part due to the freshness and enthusiasm of their discovery. Also most of their friends and relatives are more likely to be outside the community of faith.

As soon as we begin to share what we have discovered, we will encounter prejudice. Nathanael replies with more scepticism than enthusiasm. *'Can anything good come from Nazareth?'* God's special messengers emerge from the most unlikely places. Nazareth was an obscure Galilean town, of no religious significance. In a land full of holy sites associated with Old Testament events and people, Nazareth didn't even get a mention. Furthermore, since the Roman occupation it had become a garrison town, with all the associated goings-on, not to mention the idolatry their troops brought with their immorality. Taking all this into consideration, Nazareth was not considered a likely home-environment for raising God's messenger.

Philip did not try to argue Nathanael out of his objections and scepticism. He simply encouraged him to come and see for himself.

Once again Jesus assesses the character of a potential follower. In this case Jesus commends Nathanael's sincerity and honesty. He is a true Israelite, that is, one who is determined to hold on to God, while he struggles with his doubts.

Nathanael is amazed that Jesus would know so much about him at this first meeting. *'How do you know me?'* he asks. Jesus tells him that he had seen him under a fig-tree before Philip ever called him. We are not told whether Jesus 'saw' supernaturally or simply observed him from afar. Judging by Nathanael's surprise, it was almost certainly the former. Jesus is always the one who seeks before we do.

Nathanael immediately changes from disbelief, to confessing that Jesus is, *'The Son of God ... the King of Israel.'* A first-hand encounter with Jesus is apt to change people's views of him in this dramatic fashion. There must have been a twinkle in Jesus' eye when he responds to Nathanael that he hasn't seen anything yet. Jesus tells him, *'you shall see heaven open, and the angels of God ascending and descending on the Son of Man'.*

This refers to an Old Testament story which any devout Jew would recognize – that of Jacob, fleeing for his life from Esau. The Lord appeared to Jacob at the head of a stairway on which angels were travelling up and down and this vision brought great reassurance. When he awoke from his dream he declared, *'Surely the Lord is in this place, and I was not aware of it'* (Genesis 28:16). Nathanael's encounter was equally surprising. Jesus himself had become the ongoing point of contact between earth and heaven. In his company they could continue to see 'heaven opened' with the signs of the kingdom of God evident in his ministry.

Sharing God's good news does not begin with complete strangers, but with those with whom we are already in close contact and who know us intimately. Knowing the messenger is the key to delivering his message.

**Chemistry**

I remember the day we met –
How could I forget?
You provoked a reaction,
a moment of clarity so rare
that everything, for once, made perfect sense.

Why make a formula from something so special?
This is no scientific experiment,
no laboratory controlled process
that we can distil and bottle and label and sell.

We're not making pills or potions,
A daily cure-all for a sick humanity.

No. You are the Catalyst;
and together we saw a chain reaction.

I bubbled and fizzed and you
flowed over and out of me ...

Into others.

It's pure chemistry.

## day 4

# Learn as you go

Mark 1:14-20

> 'Come and be my travelling companions and I
> will turn you into fishermen of a different
> kind.' *

Peter and John had found where Jesus lived, but that was just the
beginning. Finding is seldom final. Life consists of a journey that is
marked by stages. Our life-span is divided into chapters rather than
into years. Throughout the Gospels we find Jesus and his closest
followers constantly on the move. This mobility continues in the
history of the early church as it spread from Jerusalem, throughout
Judea and Samaria and on through Lebanon, Turkey, Greece and to
Rome. Today the church of Jesus Christ must be thought of as a
people on the move. As soon as we stop moving and growing, our
individual and corporate witness suffers.

Having moved on from being John the Baptizer's disciples,
Simon Peter and John could not go back. Now their former leader
was in prison for being outspoken about Herod Antipas's illicit

relationship. His imprisonment would soon end, not in his release, but in his beheading. So they could not go back. Life is like that – we cannot return to yesterday, but must face the unfamiliar and unpredictable tomorrow.

How do we keep moving on? By keeping our witness rooted in the same message that Jesus proclaimed. All too often the good news from God has been reduced to a message of personal salvation and distorted by emphasizing life eternal that begins on the other side of the grave. By contrast, the good news announced by Jesus was that God's reign is now at hand. The long-promised time has come. In fact 'time' will never be the same again for those who enter the kingdom of God. In the words of the apostle Paul, *'If anyone is in Christ, he is a new creation'* (2 Corinthians 5:17).

The reign of God is present wherever God's will is being done in God's power. Therefore, where Jesus is present there is the kingdom, and where his followers are gathered in his name, there Jesus is present in their midst, and the kingdom continues to grow. Among his followers, who are forgiven sinners, the kingdom is imperfectly present, but in Jesus, who is the sinless Son of God, it is present untarnished and uncompromised.

Furthermore, the church lives with the tension of the 'now' and the 'not yet' of the kingdom. It lives between the times of Jesus first coming to inaugurate his kingdom and his second coming from heaven to consummate his kingdom. The church is therefore a sign and servant of the kingdom, but it is not the kingdom in all its fullness. Therefore as individuals and as a community we represent the presence of Jesus in our lives, but we also point beyond ourselves to the Jesus who inspires us and whom we seek to serve.

We can never share the good news with another person without, at the same time, being confronted ourselves with the exciting possibilities and radical demands of that message. When we hear Jesus announce, *'At last the time has come,'* we should not conclude that it has now come and gone. With each new day it comes afresh to challenge and encourage us.

Our initial response to the message entails an about-face turn, followed by stepping out in a new direction. Up till then we have been hiding and running away from God. Now we look Jesus straight in the eye to welcome his message, place our trust in him, and accept him as the Lord of our life – identifying him as the King of God's kingdom. This is the heart of Jesus' message and is consistently so throughout his earthly ministry. This is the message that inspires us to the point where we cannot refrain from sharing it. Our witness is simply the overflow of our lives, for the abundant life that Jesus made available to us cannot be contained. But it is a futile exercise to attempt to make half-full Christians overflow!

In our enthusiasm we must not over-step the mark. Ultimately, we are not the recruiters into the kingdom. It is Jesus who prepares the heart and does the inviting. This marked him out from the other Jewish rabbis of his day, whose students took the initiative in choosing their teacher. The witness is the person used by God to help make the introductions. We are not like the store salesperson that receives commissions based on our sales record! Therefore we need to relax and be ourselves in commending Christ to the world. Most of the work is done by God alone through his Spirit in the heart of the individual. There are depths in the person we cannot reach and, if we attempted to do so, we would only do damage. Our contribution is always a fraction of the whole, although it might be a vital fraction and, on occasion, the most visible part.

Jesus calls first Andrew and his brother Simon, and then Zebedee's brothers James and John, to follow him. When anyone takes those first steps in following Jesus it is good for them to do so in company, especially with people who know them well. That way we can encourage each other, hold one another accountable, and laugh at our mistakes and misunderstandings. Brothers and sisters are good at that! On our own it is all too easy to become discouraged and wander away. We can be encouraged by the fact that we don't have to wait until the end of the journey to find Christ, but that we constantly encounter him along the way.

Jesus' invitation entailed much more than an afternoon's stroll by the lakeside. It was an invitation to embark on a life-long journey, which would be life-transforming, bringing many challenges and hardships. In following Jesus they would go to many unfamiliar places, and into situations that they would not themselves have chosen. Jesus invited them to embark on a journey, not to ride a carousel.

And what would they have learned in the course of their travels with Jesus? They would see him responding to all kinds of people and would appreciate how he treated each person as a unique individual. They saw him touch lepers while everyone else shrank back terrified of becoming contaminated by even the most casual contact. They went with him into the homes of cynical critics to confront them on their own territory. They also accompanied him into the homes of people with whom society would not pass the time of day – tax-collectors who were cold-shouldered as extortioners and traitors, who were in the pocket of Rome even as they lined their own pockets. They saw his non-judgmental dealings with prostitutes, many of whom had been driven to survive in the sex industry as a last resort, having displeased their husbands for some trivial incident and been refused divorce papers. They listened to his down-to-earth teaching about the kingdom of God, which brought it within reach of the bulk of the congregation who had been disqualified by a judgmental and hypocritical religious establishment.

Those were lessons that they would never forget, because they arose directly out of experiences that were permanently lodged in their memories. But all that is still in the future. What they did hear Jesus say could be paraphrased, *'Follow me by becoming my disciples and you will learn from me how to net the fish.'*

That was language the fisherman understood – their first lesson in good communication. As they themselves responded to Jesus' invitation, they themselves became fish in Jesus' net. They were hooked for life. In following him they had to leave behind a great deal: their nets, their boat, their business, their family – in fact, everything. 'Be prepared to travel light' is good advice in any age. What is holding you back?

During the course of the next few days we will look at how Jesus approached people and how he spoke to them about the good news of the kingdom of God. We will discover that his methods were very different from the techniques and one-size-fits-all

'Be prepared to travel light' – what is holding you back?

gospel presentation with which many of us have been confronted. It is time to return to the 'Jesus way' if the community of his followers is really serious about making sense to people who have turned off or never turned on or tuned in to the greatest news of all time.

### I will follow
It's easy to follow when you know
you're off to somewhere good.
But what happens when 'follow my leader'
stops being a game, and starts getting serious?
This is no child's play, no idle journey.
Stop: look around you;
savour the sights and smells of a strange, new land.
There's no going back now.

It's hard to leave it all behind – the comforts of home,
the old, familiar landmarks, the safety of the womb.
But there's a whole new world out there,
a new language to learn,
fresh perspectives to discover.
You learn, perhaps, by unlearning;
growing, sometimes by subtraction, into the light,
fashioned in another's image.

It's easy to wonder why –
why you embarked on this whole damn thing in the first place.
But remember that first flush of excitement,
that first moment of falling in love?
It hurled you into another dimension,
and in your heart, you know this love is real.

Where to? Who knows?
The path is narrow,
and you have no A to Zen.
Instead, you've an A to Omega,
the guide of guides,
the ultimate travelling companion:
a lamp to your feet, a light to your path.

On this journey, I have learned to be humble.
Why? Because, although I'm on the Way,
further down the road than I was,
this is still a journey:
and I haven't yet arrived.

# day 5

# Make a fresh start
John 3:1-8

'How can someone my age go back to day one and start life again as a new-born?'*

From time to time we all meet devout people whose religion consists of a list of 'dos and don'ts' – with the emphasis on the 'don'ts'. They have a litmus test for everything, which they apply to the actions of other people more than to themselves. Some religious legalists live by a long and comprehensive list designed to cover every eventuality in life. Other people have a much shorter checklist to allow more leeway. Such lists, whether long or short, come with the authority of divine imperatives. Then there is another type of legalist, who simply draw up their own list representing their personal prejudices and moral code. Such legalists hear the message of Jesus as a threat rather than as good news. The grace of God presents a powerful charge that demolishes the edifice of legalism.

The story of the Pharisee who came to Jesus by night makes an instructive case-study. He was a big-time Pharisee and a member of the Jewish ruling council. He had made it right to the top of his 6,000 member religious party, with public recognition of his law-based righteousness, his encyclopaedic knowledge and his ability to judge the rights and wrongs of people's actions. He had to master 613 commandments, with the negatives outweighing the positives by 365 to 248, which is typical of this kind of religion. The Pharisees were the moral police, who were especially watchful on the Sabbath, when there were 39 special rules in operation with which they could clobber you.

Their powerful influence was not only religious and political but also economic, for they represented the rich land-owning class, whose wealth also controlled much of the business in the city. Ordinary people ran foul of them at their peril. They could have you thrown out of the synagogue, which meant more than being excommunicated from church. It also resulted in being cold-shouldered by society.

So Nicodemus was a tough challenge – far bigger than most of us will ever have to face in our attempts to make known the love of Christ. We do not know why Nicodemus waited until after dark to visit Jesus, or what prompted his call. People were reluctant to venture out because cities were not safe places after nightfall. So, in all likelihood he chose this time in order to avoid being seen. We are also left guessing whether he was acting on his own initiative, or was sent by the council to question Jesus, with a view to obtaining statements to be used against him when the time came to take legal action.

Nicodemus was diplomatic. He acknowledged Jesus as a 'rabbi', a revered teacher, sent by God. He also recognized that Jesus' authority was reinforced by his miracles, which attested to the fact that the power of God was channelled through him. Was he sincere in making these statements? Did his opening gambit represent the council's strategy or was it the private opinion of Nicodemus who said 'we' in order to hide behind the council he was representing?

Whatever the verbal manoeuvring, Jesus cut to the heart of the matter. *'I tell you the truth, no-one can see the kingdom of God unless he is born again.'* That phrase 'born again' has over the course of centuries become so familiar, been so abused and made the butt of jokes to the point where it is difficult for us to appreciate just how startling and penetrating it was on Jesus' lips. We need to step back in time to try to appreciate what it meant for Nicodemus. By so doing we will come to understand its significance for all those who are religious legalists, including those of our own day.

Jesus knew how to play the word-game of the world of political diplomacy. I believe that Nicodemus understood what Jesus was getting at when he said, *'You must be born again,'* and then reinforced it by saying, *'No-one can see the kingdom of God unless he is born again.'* Nicodemus had spent his whole life ensuring that he fulfilled the requirements of the law as expounded by its revered teachers, and did all in his power to ensure that everyone else measured up – because, until that happened, the Messiah would not come to save Israel from her oppressors and establish his kingdom on earth.

Who are the religious legalists of our day? Pray for Christ's freedom for any legalists you know.

In his probing reply, Jesus was in fact addressing Nicodemus's opening statement. He knew full well that the council he represented rejected him as an authentic rabbi, and that they attributed his miracles not to God but to the devil. He also knew that in the coming days their attitude would further harden. Nicodemus, as a representative of that council, and as a member of the Pharisaic party, had to face the fact that that he was not a front-runner on the road that led to the coming of God's kingdom, but was at the end of a cul-de-sac. There was no way forward. His whole approach was mistaken. He had to go back to day one to start all over again on a different basis. Jesus got his attention with the startling assertion he made, *'You must be born again.'* This term can also be translated 'born from above'. The double meaning is intentional and significant.

I believe that Nicodemus understood what Jesus was getting at when he replied, *'How can a man be born when he is old? ... Surely he cannot enter a second time into his mother's womb to be born!'* If we unpack that statement, we can see that in effect he was telling Jesus, *'What you are suggesting is unrealistic. It is absurd! At my time of life and in my position in society I cannot go back to day one. The cost would be too great.'*

Religious legalists have a lot of baggage to deal with. Their burdensome traditionalism and the demands they have placed on other people, which they have found so hard to live with themselves, have ensnared them. Living with double standards reinforces denial and builds walls of self-justification. They cling to their religion of good works with which they hope to earn their salvation. It is tough to be told that such an approach is worthless in the sight of God. The price of salvation is far too high for any human being to afford out of his or her own resources.

But Jesus presses home the point by making it clear to Nicodemus that he has no choice but to face the issue. To become a newborn baby means that you have to recognize your utter helplessness. Also, for the Jew, it meant to go back to the time in life when you had no rights before the law. It means becoming the little child again. The idea of being 'born again' signifies being 'born of water' – once again there is a play on words: it is the nearest thing to a real birth with the breaking of the mother's waters, but also it is a ritual washing, which signifies the need for cleansing. John the Baptizer had practised a baptism of repentance by which Jews confessed their sins and repented in preparation for God's kingdom that was at hand. He also needed to be born of God's Spirit, which John's baptism could not convey. That could only take place when the individual placed their lives into Jesus' hands.

Nicodemus, the Pharisee and council member, who controlled the lives of so many people because of his social position, had to yield control. Jesus left him to ponder the fact that, *'Flesh gives birth to flesh, but the Spirit gives birth to spirit.'* He opened his eyes to the possibility that the Spirit of God had already begun his unpredictable and unseen work. *'The wind blows wherever it pleases. You hear its sound, but you cannot tell where it comes from or where it is going. So it is with everyone born of the Spirit.'*

There is no closure to this interview. Put too much pressure on legalists and you will lose them by driving them into increasingly strident self-justification. It is hard to decide where Jesus' conversation ends and John's commentary begins. Nicodemus comes out of the night, but there is no mention of his going back into the night. Yet, intriguingly, Nicodemus is mentioned briefly two further times by John. On each of those occasions it is evident that the Spirit of God is still blowing through his life. He defends Jesus before the council, and then goes with Joseph of Arimathea to the Roman authorities to ask for Jesus' body to take it for burial. Was that day of Jesus' death the day of Nicodemus's new birth? I would like to think so.

### Born ... and born again

A human experience, a divine gift.
Something from deep down, or up above,
or from far out ...
inspires me to keep on becoming.
To distil my essence.
Patiently.
Seconds, minutes, hours.
Days, weeks, months.
Years, decades.
A lifetime, growing by addition, and then subtraction.
Dressing naked inspiration in culture, and calling it me.
Tailoring a look. Fashioning an image.
And learning to be fashioned.
I am not you, nor you me.
We are different, but not indifferent.
Apart. And a part of each other.
Reflecting and expressing what we believe and love and value.
Consummating our sacred moments, giving birth to thoughts and ideas
    and experiences, and letting them grow.
Being born and born again.

## day 6

# Why Jesus was
# sent into the world

John 3:9–21

'God did not send his Son into the world to
condemn the world, but to save the world
through him.'

Today we continue Jesus' conversation with Nicodemus who called
on Jesus under the cover of darkness. Yesterday, we saw how Jesus
emphasized that the only way forward for Nicodemus was to make a
fresh start by being born from above by God's Spirit. Of course
Nicodemus cannot backtrack, like rewinding a recording tape, but he
can start anew right where he is. Right now, such a dire course of
action is more than he is prepared to face. And he does not yet
believe that such drastic measures are called for. What was Jesus
really getting at?

In response, Jesus tells the Pharisee that he, Jesus, knows what he
is talking about. In contrast to the second-hand knowledge of the

Pharisees, his knowledge is first-hand. Their knowledge consists of what they have read, quoted and discussed, whereas Jesus' knowledge consists in what he has seen. Jesus has experienced the power of God working through him to bring forgiveness and healing. He speaks with authority because his words are the words of God, addressing the events of life on earth and our response to them. Yet the Pharisees had rejected both his reputation as a rabbi and the content of his teaching. Therefore, it is not surprising that Nicodemus struggles to come to terms with being born from above by the Spirit of God.

Because Jesus is equally at home in both spheres, he tells Nicodemus that he is just as qualified to speak of things from a heavenly perspective as from an earthly one. Furthermore, he is unique in his claims, because he has come from heaven, a sphere where no-one from earth has been allowed to enter up until this time. But through the unique mission of the Son of Man, the door of heaven is about to be opened to all who believe in Jesus.

Nicodemus must have been well aware of the concern already being expressed in the council about Jesus. They had heard about Jesus' protest at the way the temple was being misused (see John 2:12-22), turning his Father's house into a market. They had become alarmed at what they mistakenly thought to be a threat to destroy the temple.

The people of God stood under God's judgment at this moment in history just as they had under Moses' leadership in the wilderness. Then they had spoken against God and Moses for leading them into a desert where there was neither food nor water. God had punished their faithlessness by sending venomous snakes among them to bring them to acknowledge their sins (Numbers 21:4-7). Moses interceded before God who ordered him to make a snake out of bronze and fix it on a pole for all to see. Anyone bitten by a snake had to look up to the snake in order to survive (Numbers 21:8-9). Jesus here alluded to this incident when he said, *'so the Son of Man must be lifted up, that everyone who believes in him may have eternal life'*. In referring to himself being lifted up, he is anticipating his crucifixion.

At the time of Jesus' interview with Nicodemus, God's plan of salvation was still unfolding. The Spirit had not yet been given in the way that Jesus describes because the Son of Man had not yet been lifted up. It is only after Jesus has been raised from the dead and has ascended into heaven that he will bestow his Spirit that all who believe in him as Lord and Saviour might have eternal life. But events are now unfolding fast, for the plans made by God from before the foundation of the world are coming to a decisive final stage with the coming of Jesus into the world.

Jesus' ministry in Palestine is not confined to provincial significance, but is intended to impact the entire world. Such is the scope of God's love, reaching beyond the nationalism of the Jewish people. God's purpose in sending his Son is described both negatively and positively. Negatively, believing in Jesus saves us from the consequences of being separated from God's presence. Death signifies separation rather than termination. Positively, believing in Jesus ensures eternal life, which means both a new quality of life here and now as well as life without end.

The new birth is not a momentary experience but the beginning of a new way of living. Birth is intended to lead to growth. Some Christians have become so preoccupied with the new birth experience that they feel the need to be born again and again and again, which is a theological absurdity. New birth is intended to lead to growth in character so that we increasingly demonstrate the family likeness as a child of God. Elsewhere the New Testament describes the new birth as the first stage of an adoption process.

The only basis of salvation is for people to respond to the Father's love and believe that Jesus is his Son who has come into the world for the salvation of humankind. The world in no way deserves such an intervention by God. It stands under condemnation, but the **In what areas of your life is God encouraging you to change and grow?** mission of the Son is not to declare us guilty but to offer pardon to us in our guilt and to bring about a significant transformation in our lives. Not only have our lives not measured up to the standard God has set, but we have chosen to ignore, or reject outright, his provision for our salvation. From the beginning of human history we have attempted to hide from God, loving the concealment of darkness rather than welcoming the revealing and guiding light of God's truth.

Our choice is clear. Either we continue to hide in the dark or we choose to walk in the light. But the darkness, whether of our own making or of Satan's kingdom, will inevitably give way to the light of Christ, when he returns to judge the world. Such exposure comes either now as we open our arms to welcome it, or later, when we can no longer flee from it. In company with Nicodemus we are left to ponder our need to be born from above into eternal life, into the light of God's presence.

### Choice Cuts

In the marketplace of choice,
where spirituality is as cool as Richard Gere,
you can become anyone you want to be,
pick and mix a spiritual identity from the menu.
Soul food, if you like; whatever looks appetizing.

If you find yourself getting bored,
you can change the channel,
try something new.
In consumer culture, the only price to pay
Is for the self-help books,
the courses, the crystals or the Christian TV.
Cheap grace indeed.

Jesus made a choice:
he chose the narrow path,
the harder way.
Jesus made a choice: to stick to God's plan,
though he was tempted to cash it all in
to help himself.

Jesus made a choice:
he chose us.
Jesus made a choice:
to choose life,
even though it meant death on a cross.

In a world of choice,
choice cuts like a knife.

# day 7

# Conversation at the well

John 4:1–26

> 'Jesus, exhausted by his long trek, sat down by the well. It was noon, the hottest time of day, when a woman, a Samaritan, came to draw water.' *

Large numbers of people responded to Jesus in the opening months of his public ministry. He not only had a popular following in his home region of Galilee, but even in Judea, where John the Baptizer was calling the people to repentance. Jesus did not want the Pharisees to set him in opposition to his cousin, with a strategy of divide and conquer, so he decided the time had come to return north. In making this journey, he could either take the longer route, making a detour along the territory east of the Jordan river, or he could take the direct route through Samaria. When John tells us that *'he had to go through Samaria'*, he was not indicating a geographical necessity, but that he was following God's will, which was to lead to a divine appointment.

Opportunities to share our faith seldom come at times that suit our convenience. It was often the same for Jesus. When he and his disciples arrived at Jacob's well at the end of a long walk, he was relieved to rest while his disciples went into the neighbouring town of Sychar in search of food. They had already covered about 30 miles – a travel time of a day and a half – so were understandably weary, hungry and thirsty. Jesus had no sooner sat down than a solitary woman approaches the well. He had every reason to ignore her. The custom of the time dictated that men did not speak to women in a public place, and certainly not alone. Furthermore, she was a Samaritan and Jews had no dealings with this mixed-race people, regarding them as ritually unclean. There had been a simmering distrust and antagonism between them for the past 600 years with occasional outbreaks of violence.

Perhaps Jesus immediately recognized that the woman approaching him was in special need and for some reason was isolated from her village community. Why else would she be coming to the well alone, and at the hottest time of day? Women usually gathered to collect water and exchange gossip in the morning or the evening, during the cooler hours.

The woman would immediately recognize him as a Jew and feel the awkwardness of the situation. Jesus broke the heavy silence with a simple request; *'Will you give me a drink?'* This was not a ploy on his part, but rather expressed a genuine need. It is often by demonstrating grace in receiving that we find the opportunity to give. Her response exposed her surprise that she should be spoken to, and even more that a Jew would ask her for a drink, when Jews were notoriously particular in who served them and the vessel out of which that they drank. Even at the level of mundane conversation Jesus signalled an acceptance of her as a person that broke through cultural and religious barriers.

Without warning Jesus takes the conversation to another level and in so doing makes her curious about who he is and the incredible gift he could give her. The gift on offer is that of 'living water'. Once again we see Jesus' ability to relate everyday events to spiritual truths. That's a gift from God that we need to cultivate. But there are two prerequisites to receiving living water. The first is the need to know the gift of God, which is another way of speaking of the Holy Spirit. As John later makes plain in his Gospel it is the Spirit who leads us into all truth. The second is that she needs to know the true identity of the person speaking to her – for only Jesus, God's Anointed One can give this gift.

What precisely is the gift of 'living water'. For the woman, living water meant fresh, flowing water, as distinct from water from a well or cistern. Jesus is using the term figuratively to indicate the refreshing nature of his teaching and the giving of the Holy Spirit. He says that we need the Spirit in order to receive the Spirit. The paradox is deliberate, but this is no 'Catch 22' situation. Rather, it is about the initiative of God on the one hand, and the need for our free response on the other.

Was the woman's response intended to be diversionary, or was she still struggling to get onto Jesus' wavelength? Many people, in sharing their faith, make the mistake of telling people more than they want to hear, whereas Jesus made a point of telling people a little less than they wanted to hear, so that they wanted to know more. How does he think he is going to give her water when he doesn't have anything to draw it with, otherwise he would not have asked her for water in the first place? Furthermore, how come Jesus is able to produce spring water, when Jacob, their common ancestor revered by them both, had to dig this well in order to obtain water. She wants to know if the stranger is greater than their father Jacob. Was she teasing him at this stage in the conversation, I wonder?

Jesus replies by contrasting the water down the well with the water he can offer. Not only is it more fresh, but she will not have to go anywhere else for water, for it will never run dry. Even more amazingly, every person who drinks thereby becomes a spring of water, providing drink for other people who are thirsty for God. The picture is not one of isolated fountains, but of an inundation of the Holy Spirit flowing from his followers.

At this stage in the conversation the woman is still thinking in terms of literal water and of her backbreaking daily chore collecting it. Does she really believe that the stranger has a magical water supply, or is she simply stringing him along? Having arrived at an impasse in the verbal exchange, Jesus throws her off guard by introducing a very different topic. *'Go, call your husband and come back.'* She needed her husband to be present as witness before the conversation went any further for no wife could act independently of her husband. The woman responds candidly, declaring that she has no husband.

Then the woman is moved from playful perplexity to astonishment at Jesus' next statement in which he revealed his knowledge of her domestic circumstances. He informed her that he is aware that she has been married five times, two times more than allowed according to Jewish law, a standard that almost certainly applied also to the Samaritans. Society would unhesitatingly brand her an immoral woman, not to mention the man with whom she was now cohabiting. It is intriguing that Jesus dropped the subject as quickly as he raised it. It is sufficient for the woman to know that Jesus knows, and does not condemn her. Just like Jesus, his followers today must accept people just as they find them, because that was how he welcomed us.

His words as religious teacher, coupled with his supernatural knowledge that she herself could verify, were sufficient to convince her that Jesus was a prophet. Her next step is to attempt to drive a wedge between herself and Jesus by drawing attention to the fact that Jews and Samaritans worship at rival sanctuaries. The Jews worshipped in the Jerusalem temple, while the Samaritans worshipped at Mount Gerizim, where the Lord had instructed Joshua to set up a shrine. Jesus replies by insisting that where one worships is irrelevant. She was not to know that he had already declared in Jerusalem that he himself would become the new meeting place between God and humankind, replacing the temple.

The time would come shortly, he informed her, when people will worship in a new way, through the Holy Spirit who would enable them to see the truth of who Jesus really was. Only through him could people come to know God as Father, and this realization would come as they were welcomed into God's family as adopted sons and daughters. What Jesus said to this woman in anticipation of his resurrection and the giving of his Spirit remains true for all time and people. No-one comes to know God as Father except through Jesus, his Son. As she stood face to face with Jesus, the time that was coming had now arrived. She had to make a decision if she was to learn any more.

She could declare that she knew that the Messiah was coming, though her understanding of that term was different from that held by the Jews. For the latter, it meant a king like David, who would outshine him. For the Samaritans it meant a prophet like Moses, who would teach the law. Because the idea of Messiah does not have the political baggage of his own people, Jesus is able to affirm her and openly acknowledge that he was in fact the Messiah – God's special messenger.

**Think of a recent conversation you have had with an unbeliever. What can you learn from Christ's approach?**

Throughout this long interview, the longest conversation recorded in the New Testament, we see Jesus' skill, patience and persistence. The woman is given ample opportunity to speak and to influence the direction of the conversation. And we see Jesus bringing her back to the main thrust. We can learn much from Jesus to help us to become better listeners, who can engage in meaningful conversation.

### Drinking deep

Ever been dying for a drink?
Caught in the midday sun without so much as a drop;
your tongue glued to the roof of your mouth,
dry as cardboard.
Head aching, sweat dripping ...

How good it is, finally, to slake that thirst,
to find life-giving water
and drink ... and drink ... and drink ...
H2 oh – so very, very good.

Strange how everything needs it –
people, plants, animals;
earth, sea, sky.
The whole world,
just waiting for the heavens to open.

Pure, clear,
flowing, refreshing.
Cooling.
Gushing.
Bubbling.
Invigorating.
Cleansing.

Deep.

# Open your eyes

John 4:27-42

> 'Open your eyes and look at the fields!
> They are ripe for harvest.'

Jesus' disciples arrived just as his conversation with the woman at the well had reached a crucial point. They made no attempt to disguise their surprise that Jesus should be found talking to a Samaritan woman, or to discover what Jesus had been saying to her. Their silence on the matter, and the fact that they totally ignored her presence, made the woman realize that they wanted nothing to do with her. She therefore left without saying another word. But, significantly, she left her water pot, an expensive and essential household item. Does this indicate her confusion and haste in departing, or her intention to return? Or that she lost interest in everyday things when she discovered Jesus? Her desire to tell her town became more important than the expensive water pot.

As far as the disciples are concerned as soon as she was out of sight she was out of mind. They immediately focused on their own concerns. But John, in recording this incident, cleverly keeps two scenes in view. On the front-stage is Jesus and his disciples, while on the back-stage another drama is unfolding between the women and the townspeople.

Backstage, the woman is so excited by her encounter with the Jewish prophet that she issues an invitation to everyone in sight to, *'Come, see a man who told me everything I ever did. Could this be the Christ?'* Here we see the overstatement of the enthusiast! Jesus had not in fact told her *everything*; he had simply revealed his knowledge of her many husbands and present living arrangement. But she probably assumed that if he knew this much, there wasn't much else he didn't know! At least her pronouncement caught the attention of the town, who also knew her by her notoriety. In order to be an effective witness one does not need an extensive knowledge, simply a personal encounter that has at least raised the significant question, 'Could this be the Christ?' Considering who was asking the question, it was worth checking into.

Have you ever insensitively killed a conversation or made a stranger feel unwelcome in your fellowship?

A crowd emerged through the town gate towards the well to meet this intriguing stranger. Often, the most effective witness is the person who raises a question rather than the one making a dogmatic statement. As the story rapidly unfolds we will see that there is great benefit in a person coming to a decision as part of a community rather than as an isolated individual. This was especially true for a woman in first-century Palestine, and remains so today in societies with a strong sense of extended family and community.

While these spiritually significant events are taking place, Jesus' followers are concerned with more personal matters. They were urging Jesus to eat the food that they had purchased in the town. Presumably they themselves were eating their meal, unless they had already done so in the course of returning with their purchases.

Having spoken to the woman about her concern – water – he now addressed his disciples in terms relating to their preoccupation of the moment – food. He informed them that he has food to eat that they did not know about. Just like the Samaritan woman, they too misunderstood Jesus, thinking in literal rather than metaphorical terms. While he is speaking they wondered amongst themselves whether someone else has supplied him with food in their absence. But Jesus makes it clear that he is not referring to food to satisfy their physical hunger. He tells them, *'My food is to do the will of him who sent me and to finish his work.'* There is much food for thought packed into this brief statement. It raises the question whether we are energized or drained by doing God's will?

When we respond reluctantly or resentfully, we are drained by the people who cross our path. On the other hand, when our priorities are right, and our will yielded to God each day, then we will bring a positive attitude to each encounter. We have all met engaging people with whom we felt that we were the most important person in the world to them. They were genuinely interested in us and gave us their full attention. That was how Jesus was with people, so that their time with him was forever significant for them. Jesus was driven by a sense of mission, which was to do his Father's will and to finish his work.

**Are you energized or drained by doing God's will?**

But Jesus was not the good guy trying to please everybody. That way would have led to his being overwhelmed with demands. His overarching purpose was not to meet the needs of every human being who crossed his path, but to do his Father's will – no more and no less. Inevitably that means being selective in order to complete the mission that the Father had entrusted to him. It is the same for every one of us. If we do not learn this basic lesson, our lives will be littered with unfinished projects, and we will dash off in different directions without getting anywhere, or we will simply collapse in exhaustion or even become paralysed by apathy.

Not only Jesus, but his followers also need to get their eyes off themselves. Their concern should not be with food to consume but with a harvest to be gathered – now, not in four months' time. As far as the disciples were concerned Samaria represented hard and stony ground, spiritually speaking. They were reluctant to sow, so reaping was not even a consideration. In fact they regarded Samaria as more ripe for divine judgment than for a spiritual harvest.

But that was to reckon without the presence of Jesus. When he is present, seed can be sown widely and fields can ripen quickly. And if we fail to look around we are certain to miss it. When we don't expect anything to happen we are unlikely to look!

In recounting the incident John wanted to make sure that his readers got the point. Now is the time for reaping in Samaria as elsewhere. Perhaps he has in mind the evangelistic work being done by Philip, which we will read about on day 27 of our journey of faith. He was the sower, and the reapers were Peter and John, who laid hands on the converts that they might receive the Spirit. The success of the early church was dependent on the ministry of Christ himself and that of his followers whom he had sent out to spread the word.

At this point in the story the foreground and background merged with the arrival of the crowd. The woman's simple statement, despite the exaggeration, had provided the decisive motivation for the people of the town to want to check out the rest of her story, and to investigate for themselves. As they listened to him and asked him questions, they too came to believe in him, which in turn reinforced the step of faith of the woman. Her acceptance of Jesus had led to her acceptance in the community.

Such was the significance of this event that Jesus delayed his journey to spend more time with the people of Sychar. Are we also prepared for our plans to be interrupted by unscheduled events? By delaying his journey for two days, he saw a second, and even larger, wave of people responding to his message. Often, the second wave is bigger because it is reinforced by the enthusiasm of those who have themselves just encountered him. But theirs was not a second-hand faith. They had not received it in a diluted form, but with first-hand potency. Second-hand religion has little appeal. Faith that is infectious is always first-hand.

**Food for thought**

It's easy to be so hungry for a challenge
that you lose sight of what it's all about.
Sowing as many seeds as possible,
scattering yourself so thin
that, in the end, the real harvest goes unreaped.
So much busyness that the real business
of people gets forgotten.

Jesus, the bread of life,
fed the starving – by talking, yes,
by offering the living word. But also
by listening. Curious about others,
that they too might be curious about him.

Could this be the one
that was talked about by the prophets?
Taste and see, as they say, that the Lord is good!
Manna from heaven in our own wilderness;
nourishment for the journey.

Good news, once it's out there,
travels fast. The Word spreads
like wild fire.

But first it takes time. With people.

# day 9

# Healing touch

Mark 1:40–45

| 'Filled with compassion, Jesus reached out his hand and touched the man.'

Some people are sick but don't know it and, tragically, only discover when their condition has become untreatable. Others know they are sick but are in denial, attempting to ignore their symptoms. The man in the incident we are considering today falls into neither of these categories. He was acutely aware of the seriousness of his condition.

In a society where privacy was unknown you could not hide the fact of leprosy for long. If he were suffering from what today would be diagnosed as leprosy, his skin would break out in ulcerating nodules giving out a foul-smelling discharge. However, in biblical times the term 'leprosy' was used to cover a range of skin diseases, including psoriasis, which caused white scales to break out.

Once the condition became evident and it seemed as though it was permanent and spreading, the sufferer had to see the priest who served as medical examiner. If he decided that it was 'leprosy' the unfortunate individual was banished from society. From that time on he had to separate himself from all human contact, tear his clothes, and shout 'unclean' whenever another person approached him. His only company consisted of other lepers.

The leper was someone who was filled with self-loathing and was bitter against a society than shunned his company, even his family and closest friends. William Barclay, in his commentary on Mark's Gospel, records that in the Middle Ages the priest, wearing his stole and carrying a crucifix, led the leper into the church and read the burial service over him. The leper was treated by society as a person who was already dead. His suffering seemed like a living death as he was reduced to the status of a non-person. Coupled with his mental anguish was the progressive loss of feeling, the sight of his loss of limbs and the stench of untreated sores. All his senses combined to reinforce his awareness of his plight.

We may live in a country where leprosy is a disease of the past, yet there are physical conditions and mental states that still fill us with a sense of self-loathing and the need to avoid the company of others. This low self-image is often reinforced by the attitude of other people towards us, and is especially hurtful when we value their opinion of us. So, perhaps, we can identify in some measure with this man in his need, or we may be reminded of someone else whom we know who fits this description.

No wonder the leper in our story came to Jesus with such urgency, begging him on his knees. This was the act of a desperate man. He had probably heard about Jesus' healing ministry in Capernaum as well as other incidents during

**Who are the lepers of our own day? Is our attitude to them like Christ's?**

his travels around Galilee. News travels fast through small communities in close proximity to each other. We also note his humility and faith in coming to Jesus, for he has nowhere else to turn for help.

Jesus responds to him out of compassion, not simply because of the man's desperation, nor to make a theological statement that would vindicate his claims to be the Son of God. In the course of his

Gospel narrative Mark repeatedly speaks of Jesus' compassion as the motive for his healing of individuals (5:19; 8:2; 9:22; 10:47–48).

The fact that Jesus reached out and touched the leper is of special significance. The physical contact was not necessary for Jesus to heal him physically. But he did so in order that the man might be assured that he was clean. By touching the untouchable Jesus transferred the uncleanness to himself, thereby indicating that the man was no longer contagious or to be socially ostracized. It was the first human touch he had known in many days and probably in years. His healing was immediate. The change in him was dramatic. His restoration was not simply a remission, but a permanent cure.

Jesus sent him to report immediately to the priest. He would pronounce him ceremonially clean, so that he could be restored to the community. This is an appropriate response by the healed man. It expresses his gratitude to God and fulfils the requirements of the law in Deuteronomy 24:8 and Leviticus 14.

Jesus displays the tension within his own calling. He has the compassion to heal in response to urgent needs, but he also has a mission of teaching regarding the coming of God's kingdom. He has a sense of God's timing with the converging of events that would lead to his death on the cross for the sins of the world. Therefore he warns the man not to tell anyone about his cure because that would bring premature publicity. Furthermore, the needs of people for healing would swamp him so that his mission would be derailed. He would be overwhelmed by the sick who clamoured for this attention but with little interest in his mission beyond their own immediate needs. Physical healing does not necessarily lead to discipleship.

However, in his joy and relief, the former leper could not keep the news to himself. He talked to everyone, with the result that Jesus could no longer appear in public, but had to withdraw into the wilderness. Despite this, people still tracked him down and revealed his location to everyone else. Consequently Jesus was forced to restrict his healing to those individuals who came to him directly. We too can disobey from the best of possible motives. But our misplaced enthusiasm only serves to hamper and hinder the work of

Christ. Sometimes, silence is the wiser course, allowing the change
to raise questions until the time is right to make a public confession.
Speaking out of turn or too soon may close down further opportunities to tell our story at a time when people are ready to listen.

## Touching

It's so touching –
that man must be an angel.
I mean,
would you make contact
with a social leper like that,
an outcast, an embarrassment,
a festering sore on the face of our
community?

I prefer to think they can
look after themselves.
They say you can't catch Aids
by shaking hands, but I prefer to handle
life with kid gloves. It's all so delicate.

Anyway, those people bring it on themselves.
It's their lifestyle. It's so un-Christian,
and they're paying the price now, all right.
Why play God,
and interfere with divine retribution?
Why play God, indeed.

Still, I'm impressed. He doesn't make
a song and dance about it, either.
Keep it under your hat, I overheard him saying.
Don't go passing it on.

I'd like to think I deserved a little credit
if I were him.
But I'm not ... so,
who cares?

# Becoming stretcher-bearers

Mark 2:1–11

> 'When Jesus saw the faith of the four
> stretcher-bearers, he said to the paralytic,
> "Son, your sins are forgiven."' *

In these early days of ministry Jesus was immensely popular in his home province of Galilee. Wherever he went crowds gathered spontaneously. The whole town of Capernaum had gathered at the home of Simon's mother-in-law, bringing their sick to be healed and their demon-possessed to be delivered. When Jesus slipped away before dawn the next morning to find a quiet place for prayer, his close followers sought him out to inform him that everyone was looking for him. But Jesus refused to have his priorities dictated by other people's demands. He had come to teach as well as to heal and to extend his ministry to all Israel. So he travelled throughout

Galilee. Now he has returned home and as the news spreads around town the crowds gather once again.

When so many people gather together in a small town, everyone knows everyone else. But it is easy in a crowd to overlook the people who are missing. Churches experiencing sustained growth face the same issue. As long as the numbers increase, leaders can ignore the challenge and plight of those they are not reaching. They can also overlook those who are slipping quietly away because they have been ignored or nobody showed concern about the problems they were facing. When people can go missing without being missed then the church has an assimilation problem.

Some well-attended churches also face the same problems as that house in Capernaum where *'So many gathered that there was no room left, not even outside the door.'* Churches have to worry even more because they have to meet fire-regulations that place limits on occupancy! The house is full and the meeting is well under way, with the crowd hanging on Jesus' every word. Most people were simply concerned with their own spiritual appetites being satisfied.

But there are four men who have been thinking beyond themselves. They know of one person in town who couldn't be there even if he wanted to. They recognized that he needed to be there more than most. It is one thing to invite people to a meeting; it is another to care enough to go and get them. In this incident we see more than an individual deciding to do something. We see four guys taking concerted action. Whether one person enlisted the help of the other three, or the four decided together, we do not know. But they took action and achieved their goal as a team, accomplishing something beyond the strength of one person.

Let's now look at the story from the viewpoint of the paralytic. Might he have been in his helpless state so long that he had given up all hope? On the other hand, I suppose he could have pleaded with people to take him to Jesus. If he did, he was unsuccessful. He had no need to worry, because there were four guys who cared enough about him to go get him, and to carry him there. However, they encountered a problem. The crowd was so tightly packed that it became a barrier to them getting anywhere near Jesus. A 'me-first' mentality always excludes others, which often means the most needy.

The four men could have been excused if they had given up at that point and carried the paralytic home with his hopes dashed. But they refused to abandon their mission so readily. They demonstrated their determination and resourcefulness by making their way through the crowd to climb the stairway on the side of the house onto the flat roof. I have often wondered what the paralytic was saying to his stretcher-bearers as he clung to his precarious pallet and then watched them opening up the roof. I can't imagine the crowd was silent either.

Jesus must have become aware of the commotion outside at the same time as debris from the growing hole in the roof began to fall around him and shower him with dirt. Those men on the roof were determined that nothing should stop them from completing their mission. Their action challenges us about the strength of our commitment and the extent of our resourcefulness in continuing to bring people to Jesus.

**What radical action do we need to take to help someone encounter Jesus?**

Now let us imagine that we are amongst the early arrivers who managed to squeeze inside the house. The picture is full of drama and humour. What is the reaction of the homeowner to the damage being done to his property? (Did the four men return later to repair the hole?) We don't know why there are men on the roof making a hole until it is large enough for us to see the paralytic on the stretcher. At this point Jesus takes charge of the situation. Mark's observation in the story is significant: when Jesus sees *their* faith, that is, the faith of the four stretcher-bearers exercised on behalf of their friend, he speaks to the paralytic. And Jesus continues to look for people who have faith in him for their friends and are prepared to take appropriate action to remove every obstacle to their coming to him.

If the events unfolding before us are surprising, Jesus' words to the paralytic are no less so. Looking down at this helpless man lying at his feet we would have expected Jesus to say, 'Be healed!' After all he was known for his healing ministry throughout the town. Instead he said, *'Son, your sins are forgiven'*, at which a heavy silence immediately descended on the room. The expression on the faces of the theologians as well as their body language revealed their shock and disapproval. They knew that only God had the power to forgive sins, which made Jesus' claim blasphemous. Blasphemy was regarded as a capital offence among Jews of the period.

Jesus knew exactly what they were thinking. These teachers of the law were correct in the question they raised, *'Who can forgive sins but God alone?'* but were wrong in the conclusion they came to, that Jesus could make no such claim. It is this false conclusion that Jesus now challenged by posing a question, *'Which is easier: to say to the paralytic, "Your sins are forgiven," or to say, "Get up, take your mat and walk"?'* At one level, it is easier to declare forgiveness because there is no outward evidence, whereas the claim to restore movement to a paralytic is immediately verifiable.

In Jesus' ministry both forgiveness and healing are signs that God is present through him. He refers to himself as *'the Son of Man'*, a title he was to use often in the course of his ministry. It conveys his claim to be God's representative sent to achieve his saving purpose, as anticipated by the prophet Daniel. At the same time 'the Son of Man' was sufficiently ambiguous to avoid inflaming misdirected messianic passions. He had not come to instigate a political uprising, but to inaugurate a movement that would in due time present a more radical and positive challenge to the system.

On this occasion the healing of the paralytic is presented as proof that Jesus had the power to forgive sins. On hearing this, the four friends came to appreciate that Jesus could accomplish even more than they had in mind in bringing their friend. The healing is instantaneous and complete. Nerves are reconnected and muscles, atrophied through lack of use, are restored. He gets up, picks up his mat, and walks out in full view of everyone.

The crowd stands amazed as they make way for the restored man, with the comment rippling through the ranks, *'We have never seen anything like this!'* Yes, they had witnessed a spectacle, but had they heard and grasped the significance of what Jesus had said? Our sins can cripple just as severely as any physical ailment, and far more permanently. We have all seen heart-wrenching pictures of starving and diseased people, but a person crippled emotionally and destroyed morally is just as disfigured.

### Hitting the roof

He may have brought a paralysed man to his feet
and a crowd to its knees,
but still:
who was this to perform open heart surgery,
to declare that 'your sins are forgiven'?

And to suggest that faith, too,
had made old flat-on-his-back whole.
The faith, that is, of four friends,
who made another kind of hole
to reach the healer.

We thought our world was caving in
that afternoon. Turns out it was the tiles.
But it felt so strange, to see the light
and find that faith in one man
could heal from the inside out.

The Pharisees hit the roof.

# Abandoning a lucrative post

Mark 2:13-17

> 'As Jesus walked along by the Sea of Galilee
> he saw a customs officer named Levi son of
> Alphaeus sitting at the tax-collector's booth.
> "Follow me," Jesus told him, and Levi got up
> and followed him.'*

As Jesus moved around Galilee, crowds drawn from all walks of life followed him. Mostly they were the ordinary village and small-town people. But among them were Pharisees who came to monitor what was happening and to take note of points in his teaching that they could use against him.

Also among the crowds, especially in the far North Eastern region were a number of tax-collectors who made a handsome profit out of the customs dues they collected from travellers and merchants crossing from the territory governed by Philip. In addition they collected taxes from the local people on their produce and the fish they caught. These taxes were so burdensome that it was not unknown for people to flee their homes when the news got around that the tax-collectors were in the area and even for the population of whole villages to go into hiding.

Tax-collectors were hired to get results and, to ensure that they collected diligently, their own pay was based on a percentage added to the amounts they collected. The system was open to abuse and frequently led to extortion. But tax-collectors were also hated because the tax levels were fixed by their Roman overlords, so to do their work meant that you were a traitor to your own people.

The fact that they were also present in the crowd is evidence of the popularity of Jesus' teaching and that his coming to the area was regarded as an occasion not to be missed. More than that, Mark indicates that there were many tax-collectors who had begun to follow him, not only as hangers-on, but as his disciples.

Think of the kind of people who draw the crowds today. Not orators, to be sure, but artists and celebrities. Who is speaking the language of the people and addressing their concerns? Who do people want to hear from, perhaps through their songs, rap lines, or film productions? Jesus spoke the language of the people of his day in ways that entertained as well as instructed. How can we be as creative as he was to gain a hearing in our day?

Imagine the drama of this incident. Here comes Jesus, with the crowd following on his heals, en route for the next vantage point and a fresh group of hearers from the nearest town. He suddenly spots Levi and to everyone's utter amazement calls him out with a command to follow him.

This abrupt way of calling is identical to that of his call to the four fishermen to become his teachers-in-training. What an unlikely start to a movement! Who but Jesus would have begun with such an undistinguished group?

Cohesion is crucial to the success of any movement. Imagine the reaction of Peter, Andrew, James and John, to Levi joining their ranks. He represented the hated officials who ate into their profits.

On one level most of the disciples had a great deal in common, for with possibly one exception they were all from Galilee. Yet, they represented different backgrounds and personalities. Bringing together the fishermen and a tax-collector was like trying to mix oil with water. Then add Judas Iscariot (Iscariot translated means 'the dagger man'), who was probably a gang member of one of the revolutionary groups that were biding their time until the moment was right to liberate their people from Rome, and you have an explosive mixture. But with the gathering together of this motley crew you have an indication of the nature of the kingdom of God. It is a group that only the presence of Jesus could hold together.

Levi obeyed without question, just like the fishermen. In so doing he abandoned his custom's post and the lucrative living and security that it provided. In leaving his post he also left behind the protection of Rome, and immediately became vulnerable to any aggrieved person seeking revenge. Their first stopping place was significant – Levi's home. The crowd immediately divided into two groups. Levi's tax-collecting friends and other social misfits entered Levi's home while the bulk of the crowd backed away, making it clear that they did not associate with such people.

But Jesus was quite at home with the folks no-one else would have anything to do with. He had no hesitation about entering their home and being a guest at their table. In the culture of the New Testament eating together had enormous significance. It meant that you were truly one with them. His action was especially significant as a rabbi. Rabbis were the most choosy about the company they kept, and preferred to eat with people of their own kind with whom they could pursue their religious interests. Here we find Jesus doing what no other rabbi would consider for a moment.

At one level it would seem that Jesus was going against the teaching of the Hebrew Scriptures. For instance, Psalm 1 declares, *'Blessed is the man who does not walk in the counsel of the wicked or stand in the way of sinners or sit in the seat of mockers.'* The real issue, however, is not who associates with whom, but who is influencing whom? If we judge Jesus' actions by appearances or hearsay, they are likely to be misinterpreted. By associating with them he is not condoning their lifestyle but rather is among them, as a doctor among patients. But in order to be in a position to help them he did genuinely enjoy their company. He saw them as individuals not stereotypes.

When the Pharisees, who were the religious regulators and moral police of the society, saw what he was doing, they challenged his disciples as to why. But Jesus meets them head-on explaining that he has come to the people who realize they are sick and need a doctor. He can do nothing for those who profess to be as fit as a fiddle, either because they are in denial or they are deluded.

*Are there people outside the church culture that Jesus is prompting you to reach out to today?*

As we read through the Gospels we are constantly surprised by the kind of people who are eager to hear and respond to what Jesus had to say. Mostly they are the very people that the religious establishment of the day would consider beyond the social pale and not fit to mix with respectable religious people. I wonder what would happen if the followers of Jesus in our day spent more time in places and with people among whom we are so conspicuous by our absence? And if we were present, it would not be to play doctor, but as patients who have benefited so much from Jesus that we want enthusiastically to commend him to others who are sick.

### Taxing

I wouldn't be seen dead with you;
You're scum, aren't you?
Dirt, a traitor.
You rip us off,
trade us in,
You're a loser,
A loner,
A nobody.

Not like us.
Get out of here:
we don't want to know you.
You're sick;
you need help.

Jesus.
What's your game?

day 12

# Return home to your family and friends

Mark 5:1–20

> 'The man who had been demon-possessed begged to go with him. Jesus did not let him, but said, "Go home to your family and tell them how much the Lord has done for you, and how he has had mercy on you."'

Jesus and his disciples had experienced a stormy crossing on the northern part of the Sea of Galilee to arrive in the region of the Gerasenes. During the voyage he had stilled the storm by a simple word of command, demonstrating his power over nature. Now he is about to calm the inner storm of a tormented individual by commanding the evil spirits destroying this man's life to come out. The exact place where the boat made its landfall is uncertain but it was probably in the vicinity of Kersa. That location best fits the story. There were caves that could have been used as tombs where the madman lived and also a steep slope down which the pigs in our story rushed to their deaths.

This incident is one of the most remarkable stories of dramatic transformation recorded in the Gospels. The madman was beyond control. The townspeople had tried in vain to bind him with rope and then to chain him down, but each time he had broken loose. Now they lived in fear of this deranged person. The madman, for his part, was fearful of the people in the town who had caused him so much physical abuse. He had resorted to living among the tombs of the dead, sheltering in the caves in which bodies lay, knowing that the superstitious townspeople would not venture near.

There is a hint in the story that something even more macabre and sinister was going on, namely that the evil spirits within him were communing with the dead. Without a doubt he was a tormented soul, constantly crying out and cutting himself with sharp stones. If the townspeople feared him, we can only guess the anguish felt by members of his family. It is hard to imagine a more pathetic spectacle of a man than he who was an outcast from society and who could not bear to live with himself.

The madman probably saw the boat approaching land. Perhaps he had been aware of the storm that night and of the howling wind suddenly dying down. As soon as Jesus stepped out of the boat the madman approached him. But his response to Jesus was different from his reaction to other people. On this occasion there is no violent outburst; he simply fell on his knees subdued by the very presence of Jesus. At the same time he cried out in a loud voice, or rather the spirit within him protests, *'What do you want with me, Jesus, Son of the Most High God? Swear to God that you won't torture me!'* This response was remarkably similar to another confrontation between Jesus and a demon-possessed man, which on that occasion occurred in Capernaum. Whenever an evil spirit came face to face with Jesus, who was filled with the Holy Spirit, confrontation was inevitable and decisive.

Although human beings may fail to recognize who Jesus is, or choose to deny his deity, this is never a question with the demons.

They always named him publicly. But in every case the demon was silenced. Why did Jesus do this? Within this first-century cultural context, as in some traditional societies today, naming indicated taking power over a person. So Jesus immediately denounces their claim. It is difficult to differentiate between the evil spirit and the madman who is host to that spirit. But it is the man himself who pleads with Jesus, *'You won't torture me?'* That is how he perceived the treatment he had received at the hands of the townspeople.

Jesus calls on the evil spirit to depart from the tormented man. But it seems that there is a struggle going on. So Jesus follows up with a question, *'What is your name?'*, which also indicates Jesus' determination to gain control in this spiritual tug-of-war. The significant and surprising response of the spirit was, *'My name is Legion for we are many.'* In the Roman army a 'legion' amounted to 600 soldiers. So where were they to go? He was clearly a hard case of demonic infestation. The man was so emotionally shredded that he no longer knew who he was. He was driven mad by voices and uncontrollable outbursts of violence.

The evil spirits know that they have to obey Jesus' command to leave their host. But where are they to go, for spirits need a host to occupy? They plead not to be sent out of the area. Why is this? Some commentators speculate that it is because spirits are territorial while others suggest that they were communing with the dead through the man who lived among the tombs. They then beg Jesus to send them into the herd of pigs feeding on the hillside overlooking the sea. He gives them permission, with the result that the possessed pigs stampede into the water, until they all drown. Evil spirits always act to destroy what they inhabit.

What are we to make of this strange event? Clearly Jesus is more concerned for this man's restoration than for the value of a herd of pigs. The pig farmers understandably see things differently, especially because this is Gentile, pork-eating, territory. They are more concerned with the loss of their livestock. Once the story becomes known the local people plead with Jesus to leave their region. They cannot handle this manifestation of the supernatural.

Perhaps the presence of the demon-possessed individual among them was indicative of the dark spiritual climate of the region as a whole. Jesus did not intend to linger where he was not wanted. The purpose of his brief visit had apparently been accomplished.

It is important not to become overly preoccupied by the unexplained strange aspects of this story. We are dealing here with an extreme case under a unique set of circumstances. The Gospels record such incidents to make a clear point, namely, the power of Jesus over dark forces. This is very significant in a spirit-dominated culture where people lived in fear of such spirits and regularly encountered their destructive influence. You do not have to go looking for them. When they are active the evidence is clear for all to see.

Our attention should be focused on the transformation of an individual's life through the intervention of Jesus. His sense of self-worth has been restored. He

Take encouragement from the fact that Jesus has ultimate power over dark forces.

is now presented in the story as seated calmly and clothed. He is thinking straight and talking sense. What a remarkable change!

Realizing that Jesus was about to leave, and having no friends in the area, he begged to accompany Jesus and his disciples. Who could blame him? But Jesus took the unusual step of refusing his request. He is the first to be sent out as a witness, even before his disciples! He told him, *'Go home to your family and tell them how much the Lord has done for you, and how he has had mercy on you.'* Only the man himself knew the full extent of his deliverance from a tortured mind, a mutilated body and a haunted refuge.

Such was the gratitude he felt, he did not confine his witness to his family and friends, but went to each of the ten towns to tell his story, to Damascus, Raphana, Dion, Kanatha, Hippos, Capitolias, Scythopolis, Pella, Gadara and down to Philadelphia (modern Aman). We wonder whether it was this man's witness that made the people of the region so responsive to Jesus during his next visit to the Decapolis recorded by Mark at the end of chapter 7.

**Pure madness**

He was jabbering like a man possessed,
Screeching like a demon.
Pure madness, that Jesus even dared get near him.

It's not that we shouldn't help those who can't help themselves,
But some people are beyond the pale, aren't they?

We'll never quite comprehend what happened that afternoon
When the pigs squealed and hurtled over the hill.
All we know is that one man is now in possession of a peace

That surpasses all understanding;
instead of being possessed by a legion of darkness.

They say he's the Son of God; the demons, that is.
For us mere mortals, it's not that simple.
What on earth is happening? Jesus, the Son of God?!
Get out of here! You're scaring us.

# Belonging in order to believe

Matthew 16:13–28

> 'Who do people say that the Son of Man is?'
> 'But what about you?' he asked,
> 'Who do you say that I am?'

When Jesus called his original group of disciples they had a great deal to learn. The New Testament word 'disciple' means a learner of a particular kind. It is learning on the basis of a prior commitment. The sequence is the reverse of what we commonly suppose: not first believing in order to belong and then to do, but belonging and getting involved in the action in order to believe. In the course of following Jesus on a daily basis the disciples came to put their trust in him. As they identified with his mission their understanding of it grew and deepened. Gradually they came to the realization of who Jesus really was.

Throughout the first part of the Gospel the things Jesus said and did constantly raised the question, 'Who is he?' This comes out most clearly in Mark's account. His teaching had a ring of authority because he was in touch with real-life situations, exposing what was going on by his humorous portrayals and confrontational remarks. He had authority with the people because he was accessible and believable. They could feel that here was someone who understood, who was not afraid to speak out, and who 'walked the talk'. Jesus interpreted and explained the Scriptures in such a way that they had a fresh grasp of what they are all about. Unlike the Scribes and Pharisees who 'threw the book at them', he opened the book to them. In addition to his teaching they were also amazed at the miracles he performed, the claims he made, and the way he faced up to the religious authorities of his day. Wherever he went, he raised the nagging question, 'Who is this man?'

Toward the end of his time in Galilee Jesus travelled to the most northern point of his ministry to the region of Caesarea Philippi. He travelled with his group of twelve some 30 miles north of Bethsaida, a town on the northern tip of Lake Galilee in search of some peace and quiet. Jesus knew the wisdom of getting away from time to time for refreshment and reflection. The scenery was spectacular with Mount Hermon towering in background, its snow-capped peak reaching nearly 9,000 feet. But, although beautiful, this was not a holy place to Jewish eyes but a pagan place, located in Gentile territory, and famous for its grotto dedicated to the worship of the Greek god Pan. In fact it had been named *Paneas* until Jesus' time, when it was renamed in honour of Herod's son, Philip and the emperor Caesar Augustus.

Jesus began by asking his band of twelve, *'Who do people say the Son of Man is?'* 'What's the word on the street?' The title that Jesus had given himself was deliberately ambiguous. Some of his audience would associate it with the Son of Man referred to by the prophet Daniel who would come as God's representative to deliver Israel. But had he come just to set the stage or was he the principal performer on the stage of history?

Why did Jesus put this question to his disciples, when surely he knew more than they what the people were saying? He was using it as a lead in to his crunch question and to see if his disciples had any more understanding than the crowd that gathered at every opportunity. From the disciples' answer it is evident that most of the people still thought that Jesus was God's messenger to announce the coming reign of God. In other words, 'the Son of Man' was one of the prophets who had returned to earth; some got him confused with John the Baptizer, while others thought he was one of the ancient prophets like Elijah or Jeremiah. No doubt he was watching them carefully to see if they identified with any of these opinions.

Then he put his real question, *'But what about you? Who do you say that I am?'* What verdict had they come to after listening to his teaching and seeing his miracles? They could hardly have missed the puzzle that while he came to declare that the kingdom of God was at hand, most of his teaching was focused on himself! In response, Simon Peter gave a clear and unequivocal answer, *'You are the Christ, the Son of the living God.'* Simon had come to the conclusion that Jesus was more than a great prophet, but was the uniquely Anointed One sent by God to bring his reign into being. How had he arrived at this conclusion? Certainly not by consulting the religious authorities. Jesus himself had only given clues while refraining from making outright claims. No, Peter had arrived at this stunning conclusion through God's revelation to him, not just in a general sense, but with the thrill of personal realization – what we might call an 'ah-hah!' experience, or a serendipity. We all need to come to this realization. Sometimes our experience might come in the form of a sudden revelation, or from a gradual realization.

Jesus made this moment memorable for Peter by making it the occasion for a name change and to reveal to him his future role in the church: *'You are Peter.'* This is a word-play in Greek on Peter (*Petros*) and 'rock' (*petra*). It is on this confession that

**What about you? Who do you say Jesus is?**

God will build his church and Peter will be given the keys of the kingdom of heaven. As a future apostle he will become the first of the foundational rocks who had known Jesus personally and could testify to the fact that Jesus had been raised from the dead, appearing to them in person.

There is a particular rock in the English Lake District that I associate with Peter. It is a large rock called Napes Needle and it is perched on the top of a pinnacle. It is particularly difficult to climb because it wobbles. Peter himself proved to be the 'Rock that rocked'! Peter was not as firm a leader as he believed himself to be. His brave declaration that he would never deny his Lord turned out to be bluster when the test caught him off guard. And later, as a church leader, he struggled when non-Jews began to respond in significant numbers. Even foundation pillars of the church shake from time to time.

Jesus here declares his intention to build his church no matter how strong the opposition. His promise that the Gates of Hades will not overcome it let us know that death threats and persecution will not succeed in defying and dismantling his church. Nearly two thousand years of church history have proved him right, especially in the experience of the church since the second half of the last century. It is only when churches have become weakened from within or have tried to advance through military conquest and political manoeuvring that they have been forced into retreat or simply fallen apart.

Peter is given here the keys of the kingdom on the basis of his confession that Jesus was God's anointed messenger, the Son of the living God. The person who carries the keys holds authority. But Peter is not the only one who held this office. Jesus teaches later in Matthew's Gospel that brothers who went to correct recalcitrant believers exercised a ministry of 'binding and loosing'. If the offenders persisted, then they would be locked out of fellowship, but if they sought forgiveness from their brother or sister, they will be let in. Their judgment is not simply on the human level, it is one with which heaven concurs.

Although everyone is welcome, only those who make the same confession as Peter truly belong. Yet, this should not lead those who belong to a superior attitude. Peter still had much to learn, as did the other eleven followers of Jesus. That is why Jesus told them not to spread it abroad that he was the Christ. They did not fully understand yet what that title implied, and to make a public announcement would merely fuel the nationalistic expectations that were smouldering throughout the land. It would not have taken much to fan those into flame with catastrophic consequences for the nation.

Jesus' disciples had grasped the fact that he was indeed the Anointed One from God. But like so many people who longed for God to liberate his people, they had very different ideas from Jesus. He tried to correct their false notions by telling them plainly that he was under divine constraint to begin his journey to Jerusalem, not as a political liberator, but to suffer many things at the hands of the religious authorities and there to be killed. But, listen on, his death would not be the end, for on the third day he would rise again.

Such a scenario was unthinkable to the disciples, and the ever-impetuous Peter protested, *'This shall never happen to you!'* In response Jesus let him know in the strongest terms that he is out of order: *'Get behind me, Satan!'* The one who had just been declared a building block of faith has immediately become a stumbling block to faith. There is no avoiding this central truth, that salvation is through suffering – the suffering of the Son of God who was soon to die for the sins of the world.

But there was more to come. Not only did the disciples have to face the inevitability of Jesus' death, they also had to be prepared to die themselves. Followers of Jesus can no longer live for themselves, but must learn to deny themselves and take up their cross in order to follow him. Luke's version of the incident adds that we must take up our cross *daily.* Symbolically, this means that we must die to our selfish ambitions, and lay aside our priorities. Responding to Jesus means a total reordering of life's priorities and seeking first the kingdom of God. It is a poor exchange to lose your soul in order to gain the world. The ultimate indignity is to seek our sense of identity by wearing a designer label. The story is told of a group of friends standing at the graveside of a multimillionaire. One friend enquired of the person at his side, 'How much did he leave?' 'Everything,' he replied, 'including himself, for he had become nothing apart from his wealth.'

### Who am I?

Who do you say that I am?
How can you tell?
Just by looking?

Am I the clothes that I wear?
The car that I drive?
The labels that I sport?
The surface appearance,
the veneer of respectability?

What makes you so special, anyway?
You've bought into the brand –
I can see that.
You're a believer because you have the bumper sticker
and the fish badge on your lapel.
Part of the club.
Must I really be like you to join the club?

What exactly does it mean to be branded?
To take the mark?
To bear the scar?
How do I take up my cross
when you've strung it round your neck
in a fashionable silver chain?

Who did they say that HE was?
The Christ? The Messiah?
And how, exactly, could they tell?

Just by looking?

## day 14

# Obstacles to progress

Mark 10:17–31

> ' "Go, sell everything you have and give to
> the poor ... Then come, follow me."
> He went away sad, because he had great
> wealth.'

We live in a market-driven society that is fuelled by materialism.
Those who have technical knowledge and a head for business can
reap tremendous rewards. Today, there are more twenty-something
millionaires than ever before. But the majority of us are not so smart
or fortunate. By the standards of our society we may not feel very
wealthy, but in terms of the standard of living of the rest of the
world, most of us are in the top 10%.

Mark tells us that a man came running up to Jesus. Matthew, in
his account of the same incident, adds that he is a 'young man',
while Luke informs us that he is a 'ruler', which meant that he held
a prominent position in the local synagogue and was probably a
Pharisee. All three accounts make the point that he was very rich. He

was in the top 1% in terms of power and privilege. But like many a person who has reached the top of the ladder (or was born there), he was dissatisfied. Deep within his heart there was an empty void that his abundant material resources could not fill. On the outside he was very rich, whereas on the inside he was desperately poor. He isn't the only person in that condition.

This young man was evidently earnest in his approach to Jesus, for rich people in New Testament times didn't run! Such exertion was considered beneath their dignity. The day of the track-suited, health-conscious jogger was far in the future. As soon as he caught up with Jesus, he fell on his face, not so much out of exhaustion as to show respect and reverence. He immediately blurted out his question. His coming straight to the point provides yet another indication of his eagerness. *'Good teacher, what must I do to inherit eternal life?'*

His question was right on target. But what did he have in mind? He wanted to know how he could secure his place (hopefully, a prominent one) when the prophecies were fulfilled and God's kingdom was established through the Jewish nation. For during those days there were rising expectations that God might intervene in a spectacular way on behalf of his people. His wealth was evidence of God's blessing on his life and his position in the synagogue was evidence of Jewish society's approval. Was there something else? A detail that he had overlooked?

In response to this young man's question, Jesus cut through his defences with the skilful precision of a surgeon. *'Why do you call me good? No-one is good – except God alone.'* In saying this he was not correcting the man for thinking too highly of him. Rather he was challenging his superficiality. If he was going to get an answer to his question, he would need to relate to Jesus in an appropriate way. Flattery would get him nowhere. He had to know what 'good' really meant in the eyes of God, whose standards are of a different order than ours.

As a religious leader and devout Jew, Jesus could be assured that this young man would know the Ten Commandments. So he checks off a few at random. Number 6: do not murder. Number 7: do not commit adultery. Number 8: do not steal. Number 9: do not defraud. Number 5: Honour your father and mother. Test over. Score: five points out of five. *'Teacher,'* (he remembered to drop the 'good' this time), *'... all these I have kept since I was a boy.'*

But what about the first four commandments about worshipping the one true God and keeping the Sabbath? He felt confident that he could maintain a perfect score. But to his amazement Jesus took another tack that completely blind-sided him. In so doing, Jesus knew that the young man was going to find it difficult in the extreme to hear what he was about to say. We can be thankful to Mark for supplying the significant statement in his account of this incident that *'Jesus looked at him and loved him.'* There was no hint of harsh condemnation, but rather of earnest pleading. It is with the same look and tone of voice that he speaks to each of us when he has to address a core issue in our lives.

*'One thing you lack ...'* I wonder, did Jesus pause then for a moment to get his full attention? *'Go, sell everything you have and give to the poor, and you will have treasure in heaven. Then come, follow me.'* In that moment Jesus publicly exposed the young man's underlying problem. His treasure had become his ball-and-chain, and its storeroom his prison house. He could not follow Jesus until he rid himself of that burden. He

**What is Jesus asking you to give up, or give away, so that you can be more devoted to him?**

had to face the choice of whether his trust was in Christ or in his possessions.

Then he made the greatest miscalculation of his life in placing the value of his earthly treasure above that of heavenly treasure. This rich man who was so poor inside became the wise man who revealed himself to be so foolish. *'At this the man's face fell. He went away sad, because he had great wealth.'* He wasn't prepared to let go. The goodness in Jesus presented too radical a challenge.

What saddened the rich young ruler shocked the followers of Jesus, for they also believed that riches were an evidence of the blessing and favour of God. They thought that the pious rich were the privileged few, a widely held view that Jesus decisively challenged with a touch of humour. He painted a ludicrous picture of a camel, the largest animal in the Near East trying to get through a hole the size of the eye of a needle. The lesson is as clear as it is startling. Rich people cannot worm their way into the kingdom of heaven. It simply cannot be done. Their wealth cannot buy them a ticket and their influence cannot help them by-pass the requirements. It is not only those things in our lives that we know shouldn't be there that will hold us back, but sometimes even the precious things that we value most. And, sometimes, they are the most difficult of all to deal with.

But from this call to abandon our trust in possessions, we should not conclude that we are expected to grovel in poverty or to feel somehow deprived of the good things in life. Jesus made it clear that in the end, even as we accompany him along life's way, we receive more than we have ever given up. And we can enjoy them more, because what God now gives us to possess will never possess us.

The young man in the story – so rich and yet so poor, so wise and yet so foolish – began so near but tragically ended up so far away from God. This incident provides a warning to all of us. Yet even this story is not without a ray of hope. The fact that he had seen Jesus' look of love and walked away sad means that he would be haunted by that gaze, and that he now knew the reason for his empty heart. I like to think that he eventually returned and put his life back on track. We cannot be sure about the young man, but we can be sure about our own response.

### Lifestyle choice

Are you sitting comfortably?
And if so, are you really ready
for the moral of this story?

When was it that we began to make
our faith a lifestyle choice,

one among many on today's
spiritual smorgasbord?

Do you buy into Christianity?
Or do you count the cost?
Have we all sold out?
Or can we, even now, be redeemed?

We have a choice:
not to possess, but to be possessed –
by our consumer durables, our fashions, our fancies ...
or by the One who paid the ultimate price.

Purchased by blood, sweat and tears,
in the sale of the century.
I am taking myself off the market:
For good.

## day 15

# A grandstand view
Luke 19:1–10

'Come down right away. My heavenly father insists I am to stay at your house today.'*

People pay high prices to get a grandstand seat with an unobstructed view. The individual in our story got his perch for free. His aim was a modest one. He simply wanted a glimpse of Jesus passing through Jericho near the end of his long trek from Galilee to Jerusalem. Whether or not Zacchaeus realized it, this was his one and only opportunity. At least having seen the one talked about by his fellow tax-collectors would satisfy his curiosity. Jesus was that unusual rabbi, who took the trouble to befriend tax-collectors without regard for what people thought.

Friends outside of their own tight circle were few and far between, at least among their own race. Tax-collectors were hated and despised. Hated because they were unscrupulous, milking the people for all they could get. Their income represented the difference between the amount they were able to collect, and that which they handed over to the Roman overlords. And they were despised, because they were serving the occupying forces, acting as their lackeys. Roman taxation was a crushing burden, felt at all levels of society. Therefore to be a tax-collector meant that you made a lot of enemies. That would make them nervous of crowds. And a chief tax-collector would make even more enemies as the middleman who wanted his cut of the takings; hated as much by the tax-collectors under him as by the people who had to meet their demands. I reckon that Zacchaeus ran ahead, not just because his view would be blocked by the crowd because he was so short, but also to remain inconspicuous.

Safe in the sturdy sycamore-fig tree, with its spreading branches and large leaves, he would be able to see without being seen. Or so he thought. An unforeseen dramatic turn of events was about to take place, for when Jesus arrived at the spot, he looked up, and called Zacchaeus by name. How did Jesus know his name? Had Zacchaeus's reputation spread far and wide, or did Jesus know it by revelation? The story doesn't supply the information. But frequently when God calls an individual it is personal and specific. That's as true today as it was then.

Zacchaeus had wanted simply to remain an anonymous spectator. But Jesus ordered him down immediately with the astonishing statement, *'I must stay at your house today.'* That was the last thing the crowd expected to hear from Jesus. In their estimation some resounding rebuke would have been more appropriate. They would rather have seen Zacchaeus publicly vilified. They could not contain their resentment at Jesus honouring a crook by inviting himself to the place that most of them avoided at all costs.

Jesus says *'must'*. This tells us this is no momentary impulse, but the outworking of a divine plan. And the Lord has more in mind for us than we are usually aware of! This is no isolated incident in the life of Zacchaeus, but one of a series of linked events. Jesus also says *'today'*. This emphasizes that this is a special moment that urgently demands a response. 'Today' is a word that is linked to salvation elsewhere in the Bible. The apostle Paul writes to the church in

Corinth: *'I tell you, now is the time of God's favour, now is the day of salvation'* (2 Corinthians 6:2).

In accompanying the chief tax-collector to his home Jesus was not condoning his lifestyle. His unconditional love was always with a view to bringing about a radical transformation. The change came about through the encounter, not through a sermon or even a conversation.

Zacchaeus could hardly believe what he had just heard. Face to face with Jesus and surrounded by a hostile crowd, he blurted out that he will give half of his possessions to the poor. Suddenly, those possessions had become a burden and a barrier from which he must find release. And he follows this up with a declaration of his intention to pay back fourfold anything he has cheated out of people. The reaction of the crowd is left to our imagination. The curtain comes down on the incident as Jesus declares, *'Today salvation has come to this house.'* His public declaration was clear evidence of his repentance for his past life, and went far beyond what the law of the Jews required, which was calculated at the amount taken plus one fifth. The spirit of the good news of Jesus always goes beyond the letter of the law.

Jesus declared Zacchaeus, the social outcast among his people, to be a son of Abraham, not simply by racial decent, but because of his wholehearted response to the word of God. He was a spiritual descendent of Abraham. His trust was no longer in the wealth that he had accumulated, but in the guest he had welcomed. As a result he would have to learn to depend on God as never before. He had thought he was the one seeking Jesus, whereas the fact of the matter was that Jesus had been seeking him. This was Jesus' central purpose – to seek those for whom society and self had given up all hope.

The Son of Man came to seek relentlessly until he found those who were

**Think of a time when Jesus sought you out, even though you might have been hiding from him, and give thanks.**

lost, that is, those who were excluded or who considered themselves beyond rescue. The hidden seeker became the one who was openly sought by the Lord. What a turnaround! The Salvation Army is right when they describe salvation as 'from the guttermost to the uttermost'.

### Today is the greatest

Today is the greatest day there's ever been;
a moment of presence,
putting paid to the past,
and investing in the future.

The presence of one who knows my name,
for all the right reasons, not the wrong ones.
The presence of one who will talk with me,
no matter what the rest say.

No matter how taxing I've been,
the tables are turned.

Those who owed me, I now owe;
thanks to a debt that I find was paid for me.
My life was always in the balance;
but he said it was worth something,
something more than cash,
more than all the cash in the world.

You have to give him credit –
for he gave it first to us.

To me. To you.

Today is the greatest.

## day 16

# Sight to the blind

Mark 10:46–52

> 'Many people in the crowd ticked him off,
> telling him in no uncertain terms to be quiet,
> but he shouted out all the more.'*

So much religion today is casual and occasional. It is a religion of convenience. Some describe it as 'boutique' religion or religion as an 'accessory' to life. Today's incident tells a very different story.

Jesus had reached the last stage of his long journey from Caesarea Philippi to Jerusalem. He was now just 15 miles from his destination. Passover was but a few days away, when his 'hour' would come, his appointment with destiny, when his work on earth would reach its earthshaking climax. Jericho at that time was a seething mass of humanity. There were the pilgrims who were going to this greatest of the annual festivals. Among them were thousands of priests preparing to make their journey to serve in the temple, when some 20,000 would be on duty (26 times the normal complement). Lining the Jerusalem road were crowds of onlookers consisting of those who were unable to make the journey and those who would be leaving later. As people became aware that Jesus was also passing through they no doubt swelled in their numbers. Emotions ran high among them after Jesus had snubbed the religious authorities by publicly inviting himself to the home of Zacchaeus the chief tax-collector in the town. The crowd was as divided as rival fans at a sports stadium.

As some recognized Jesus approaching, the buzz in the crowd alerted the blind man that now was his opportunity. As with Zacchaeus, it was now or never. But the blind man was driven by far more than curiosity – he was driven by desperation. He must not miss his chance, so he cried out in order to be heard over the buzz and bustle of the crowd around him. He had to attract Jesus' attention. In fact he need not have worried, for Jesus always hears cries from the heart.

**What are your cries from the heart today? Be assured that Jesus hears them.**

A few weeks ago I sat with a young man with spiked hair, and pierced eyebrows, who told me of his cry of desperation. Two of his close friends had died through heroine addiction, and he had been scared out of his mind when another friend had a bad trip after taking Speed. He cried out to God, who met him and Jesus turned his life around. Today he ministers to young people who are shackled in the same lifestyle that had bound him and from which Jesus had released him.

The attempts by the crowd to silence him simply provoked him to shout even louder. The crowds around us can be very intimidating unless we choose to ignore their unsympathetic and hostile voices. *'Son of David, have mercy on me!'* What preconceptions did he have regarding Jesus? He probably bought into the popular view that the Son of David was the Messiah who was to bring political liberation for Israel. He still had a lot to learn, for Jesus didn't come as a popular hero. But we don't have to have our theology straight for Jesus to hear our cry. The fundamental need is to identify Jesus and to exercise faith in him. It is in relationship with him and in company with the community of his followers that our beliefs get straightened out!

It is significant that Jesus initially addressed the crowd and not the blind man directly, ordering them to *'Call him.'* Those that a few moments ago tried to silence him now had to summon him. The blind man now heard kinder voices, perhaps the disciples of Jesus and sympathizers in the crowd, who encouraged him to take heart and to get up because Jesus was calling him. The blind man's response was both instant and urgent. He even threw off his cloak, risking it being whisked away by someone in the crowd, so that he wouldn't lose a moment. Nothing would hinder his response.

When Jesus asked him what he wanted him to do for him, the blind man did not hesitate. He came straight to the point: *'Rabbi, I want to see.'* Jesus must have been aware of this person's need, as he is with each one of us, but he wanted to hear him name it, as he does us. In his response, the blind man revealed that his desperation was not driven by demand but by faith – an important distinction.

Jesus had come to open the eyes of the spiritually blind, in order that they might see and follow him. This was the response of the physically blind man. He did not simply turn away to live a self-centred life. That is not the way to be made well. We are not well unless we are whole. Completeness and fulfilment only come as we embark on a life committed to Jesus as Saviour and Lord. It is significant that the blind man in this story is not nameless, but is identified as Bartimaeus, known to the Jerusalem church as a follower of Jesus. Not only was he delivered from physical darkness, but from spiritual darkness, in order that he might walk in the light of God.

**Believing is seeing**
Focus.

'An eye for an eye', they used to say;
But I can see now that I am forgiven.

Focus.

Someone spoke of this man being light;
if that is the case, I have seen it.

Focus.

In each sunset, in every face, in every bird that flies,
I trace the beauty of a Creator, who trod earth,
drew lines in the sand, got his hands and feet dirty.

Focus.

Dirt browns, yellows, reds, blues, magentas,
blacks, whites –
shades of a spectrum he dreamed into being.
What a sight:
the beauty of difference, the uniqueness of individuality –
painted, projected, dispersed, radiated and
Helping me to see.

Focus.

He made me see, for the first time,
and, for the first time, it made sense;
the scales fell from my eyes,
and the first thing I saw ...?

Focus.

The human face of love itself,
staring, curious, dirty, tired;
not at all what I'd expected
When I tried to summon visions of heavenly beauty
from the everlasting darkness.

Focus.

The first thing I saw was his face,
and the rest followed.
I followed.
And for the first time in my life,
it all came into

Focus.

## day 17

# Extravagant
# devotion

Mark 14:1-11

'I tell you the truth, wherever the gospel is
preached throughout the world, what she has
done will also be told, in memory of her.'

It is one thing to follow Christ, but what are our motives in taking
that step? We are faced with this question in today's incident. It is
two days away from Passover and the Feast of Unleavened Bread,
and the sequence of events leading to Jesus' arrest and crucifixion
are beginning to unfold. During the week beginning with Jesus'
triumphal entry into Jerusalem on Palm Sunday he had been teaching
each day in the temple, and retiring to Bethany each evening to stay
at the home of Simon the leper. We know nothing more about his
host, but it was likely that he was one of those healed by Jesus and
was now responding in gratitude by offering hospitality.

While reclining at the table for a meal, they would have been on the floor supported by cushions. A woman entered and, to everyone's amazement, took a sealed alabaster jar and broke it open to pour expensive perfume on Jesus' head and feet. Who was this woman? We have to turn to John's account to find out. He informs us that it is none other than Mary, the sister of Martha and her brother Lazarus. Her outpouring of sacrificial love was in gratitude for the teaching Jesus had given her in her home and for restoring her brother to life. The nard with which she anointed Jesus was imported from India and very costly, amounting to a year's wages. In all likelihood, the semi-transparent alabaster jar with its precious contents was an heirloom. But devotion is not calculating and Mary did not consider her action as a sacrifice. It was a spontaneous expression of love.

During this final week of Jesus' life it is the female disciples who come to the fore. They are the ones who gathered at the foot of the cross and who went early to the tomb to anoint his body. In contrast to the devotion of Mary we find the male disciples all critical of her actions. For them, any show of extravagance displayed during the Passover season was highly inappropriate, as it was regarded as a time of giving to the poor. But they desert Jesus at his time of need. Peter follows at a safe distance and then denies that he is a disciple of Jesus when challenged by a servant girl. None is available to carry Jesus' cross when he fell exhausted to the ground.

John's account adds a further detail that helps explain the harshness of the rebuke the disciples gave Mary. Suddenly realizing that she has no towel to mop up the excess of perfume, she unbraids her hair to wipe Jesus' feet. They regard such an action as highly inappropriate! But Jesus comes to her defence, telling them to leave her alone. *'She has done a beautiful thing to me.'* What critics dismiss as a wasteful gesture, Jesus valued as entirely appropriate. Her anointing of his body was a prophetic act preparing him for his burial. Mary did not realize at that moment the significance of her actions. This will be one of the last opportunities to express devotion in this manner, for Jesus would soon be taken away from them.

Jesus challenged their critical spirit on two fronts. In the first place, there was nothing to stop them expressing their generosity to the poor, who are always present, so they didn't have to wait for a special opportunity. Criticism and hypocrisy are seldom far apart. In fact one of the disciples, namely Judas, was a dishonest treasurer who had been siphoning-off funds. Second, Jesus declared that her actions would be held up as an example of true devotion to future generations wherever the gospel is preached throughout the world. No action on the part of any of the male disciples is honoured in such terms. Those words must have stung the disciples as they examined their own hearts at that moment and later when they recollected their regrettable responses to the events of that tumultuous week.

In a male dominated society like that of the first century, women do not frequently come into the foreground in the Gospel narrative. Yet on each occasion their appearance was highly significant, and Jesus' response to them was gentle and caring, while always forthright. He was never condescending or demeaning. I once asked a student who was prominent in the pop music culture what brought him to faith in Christ. His response was significant. He said, 'While we were on tour I read a number of religious books and finally came around to reading the Gospels. I was drawn to Christ by the way he dealt with women. We were rough on women.'

Behind the criticism of the disciples was the more destructive attitude of Judas. Jesus' response to Mary's devotion was the last straw. He was not prepared to align himself any longer with what he judged to be a failed cause. Judas now decided to betray Jesus to the authorities whom he knew were seeking an opportunity to arrest him. With each passing day the Jewish leaders were becoming more nervous as Jesus taught the crowds in the temple, gathering in their thousands in preparation for the feast. Should trouble occur at this peak season their Roman overlords would place their own positions in jeopardy. All along Judas had been motivated by self-interest. When he finally realized that the kingdom Jesus came to establish was not going to secure him a future among the privileged and powerful, the time had come to break rank.

Some have twisted Jesus' words referring to the poor being always with us to defend their extravagant church-building programmes and other projects. Their implication is that as the poor are always with us we can therefore ignore them. But the real issue is the extent of our devotion to Jesus personally. His statement should never be used to divert attention from the pressing needs of the poor – the very people who were the focus of so much of Jesus' ministry.

The needs of the poor are even more pressing in our own day. The world population is so much larger, the gap between rich and poor so much greater, and the mass migration of people from the countryside into the cities, and out of famine-stricken areas and war zones, is on a much larger scale than ever before. How then can we express our sacrificial devotion to Christ and to the world he came to save today?

> How can we express our sacrificial devotion to Christ and to the world he came to save today?

## Perfect scents
What can you give the one who has everything?
It's not easy to find a gift when someone's so hard to buy for;
searching the shops in vain for something that might express
your gratitude for a relationship, your love for the things they've done,
a symbol of the overflow of your heart.

What can you give the one who has given you everything?
Who has breathed life into your family, brought meaning to your
    journey;
who has treated you as you, called you by name,
demonstrated a strange kind of love when you're not used to being
    treated
like a fully human being?

What would your gratitude look like, when it's too big to wrap?
When you've never tasted such love before?

How does it feel, when nothing you've felt before comes close?
What sound would it make, when words just aren't enough?
How would it smell?

Like the most expensive perfume, filling a room,
stunning a crowd, embarrassing bystanders,
pouring uncontrollably, extravagantly,
abundantly ... ? Like the smell of fear
and the smell of joy all rolled into one?
Like the scent of excitement, anticipation,
dread, love, honesty, vulnerability ... ?

There's no going back
When you've poured out your very being
In an act of extravagant love.

day 18

# A short walk

Luke 24:13-35

> 'Jesus himself came up and walked along with them; but they were kept from recognising him.'

The journey of life consists of many short walks over familiar ground, as well as long journeys to places we have never visited before. It is all too easy to discount the dull routines and only expect to find God in the course of some exciting new adventure. A pilgrimage is about finding the Lord along the way and not having to wait until we have reached our destination.

Today's encounter concerns two individuals. One is named Cleopas and the other, whose name is not recorded, may have been his wife Mary, who had stood with the other women near the cross of Christ (John 19:25). The Feast of Passover was ended and they were taking a short walk from Jerusalem to Emmaus, a distance of seven miles, which the two must have walked many times to worship at the temple, to go to the market and to visit friends.

Only this occasion was different. They were more subdued than usual. 'Devastated' would be a more accurate description of their mood. They were deep in conversation about the events of the weekend, and were recalling the yelling crowds who had called for the release of robber Barabbas at the same time that they demanded the death of their hero, Jesus. They recalled the heart-wrenching sight of Jesus staggering under the weight of his cross as he was dragged in the procession to the site of his public execution. They had watched their hero die an agonizing death, surrounded by jeering crowds and callous executioners. With his death their hopes were dashed.

But they were trying to make sense of the strange reports of women who had visited his tomb early that morning in order to embalm his body, only to find it was no longer there. They had also reported that an angel had appeared to them announcing that Jesus' body was gone not because it had been removed, but because he was alive. They dared not pin their hopes on the testimony of the women for fear that they would only be dashed once more. The road was so familiar and their conversation was so intense that they were only dimly aware of what was going on around them.

How is our day so far and what does our schedule look like? Is it full of the same routines and familiar stuff? Or perhaps, like the two individuals in our story, our hopes have been dashed. Our heads are down and our feet are heavy under the weight of disappointment or disillusionment. We have given ourselves to some great cause, but the outcome is far from what we anticipated. 'Why bother any more?' we ask ourselves. By walking alongside the two on the road to Emmaus we can find some encouragement and be surprised by their unanticipated encounter with Jesus.

It all began when an apparent stranger came alongside and fell in step – but they were kept from recognizing that it was Jesus, the very one they had been talking about. There are times when we do not recognize his presence at our side, not necessarily because we are too preoccupied to notice, but because God has dropped the curtain and will only raise it when the moment is right – when he is ready and can see that we are responsive.

As happened so often, Jesus opened up the conversation by asking a question. Statements are more likely to close a conversation down. He asks them what they are discussing. Not that he might be informed but that they might express their feelings. They misinterpreted his question, revealing a surprising ignorance. *'Are you only a visitor to Jerusalem and do not know the things that have happened there in these days?'* But far from being ignorant of the facts, Jesus had been the central figure in the drama.

Jesus' second question is simply an invitation for them to share what was on their heavy hearts. Like many other people in Israel they had regarded Jesus of Nazareth as God's messenger to the nation. His divine power was evident in both his words as well as in the deeds he performed. But they had taken it a significant step further. They had placed their confidence in him as the Great Prophet who would secure Israel's favour with God and rescue the nation from her oppressors. Then their hopes were shattered when the chief rulers had turned against him and delivered him to the Roman overlords.

But their story didn't end there. They told him about the report they had heard from the women of their company before leaving the city, and how some of the disciples had been to the tomb to check out their story. They had hoped it was true, but now their hopes had evaporated because it was the third day – the time when in Jewish thinking the soul left the body, and when time ran out for Jesus' puzzling sayings to be fulfilled.

Having heard their version of the events, Jesus challenges them regarding their downcast spirits. They had heavy hearts because they were *'slow of heart to believe all that the prophets have spoken'*. As they walked alongside Jesus, he linked together the isolated state-ments from Moses and the Prophets, covering the whole of the Scriptures, showing their fulfilment in his own life through his ministry, suffering and vindication by God in raising him from the dead.

As the connections were made so the power flowed. The sparks of understanding flew with greater frequency and their hearts burned within them. We too can read things in the Bible that don't make much sense at the time, or that we promptly forget about in the midst of a crisis. How easy it is to fail to make the connection, but once the link is established the power flows! May our hearts be warmed afresh today as Jesus draws alongside us to reveal even more of himself through his Word and in the circumstances of our life.

**Make conscious moments today to recognize Jesus' presence alongside you, and give thanks.**

Often God's revelation begins with the warming of the heart, signifying an awareness of God's presence in our midst. But it is something difficult to express in words. Encounters can defy adequate description. Yet, at the same time, we must give expression to an overflowing heart by praying to God and sharing with others.

So impressed were Cleopas and his companion by this stranger who had opened their eyes to the Scriptures like no other teacher, that they invited him to their home for an evening meal. Jesus does not force his presence on anyone. He knocks on the door of our hearts. He does not barge in. Incredibly, the two still had no idea who he was. They were not alone amongst his followers to fail to recognize Jesus in his resurrection body. It was not until he took over the role of host at the meal table, as rabbi, and blessed and broke the bread, that their eyes were opened and they recognized him.

On a number of occasions during the forty days between his resurrection and ascension into heaven, Jesus unexpectedly appeared among the disciples while they were at a meal. His words and actions tied in to the Last Supper, which anticipated his death and resurrection. Now his actions were both a memorial of those events and a prophetic anticipation of the Great Banquet that they will enjoy in his presence at the end of time. They linked together the Messiah as revealed in the Scriptures with Jesus of Nazareth who was now in their presence. Two thousand years later our faith is sustained by the book in which Jesus is revealed and the table of fellowship where he is encountered afresh. But to this point his appearances were fleeting, for his Spirit had not yet been fully given to the disciples because he had not yet been glorified in heaven.

Those who have encountered the risen Lord lose no time in sharing their experience. That very night they returned to convey their news to the followers of Jesus huddled in Jerusalem. On arrival they discovered that they were all still together, and that their account confirmed the story of Peter, to whom the Lord had also appeared. The weary walk of Cleopas and his companion had indeed turned into an unforgettable wonder walk.

**Where was God?**
Where was God?
When it all began to go wrong?
When I cried out?
When I was frightened?
When I was ill?
When I was commuting every day and bored out of my skull –
when the journey seemed long,
the road never-ending?

Where was God in the poverty?
In the famine?
On September 11th?
In the crippling flow of global capital?
Among the drug-users?
The Aids sufferers?
Amid the carnage wrought by a suicide bomber?

He was forgotten.
Abandoned
along with the worst of them.

Jesus moved into the neighbourhood.
Felt pain.
Chose a lonely path.

Ate with sinners.
Wept with losers.
Drank with scum.
Lived with outcasts.
Died with thieves.

Walked with the downcast.
Journeyed with the hopeless.
Talked with the disillusioned.
Broke bread with the hungry.
Revealed himself to the blind.
Comforted the abandoned.
Empowered the powerless.
Taught the ignorant.

Where was Immanuel?
God was with us;
all the time.
Where was Immanuel?
God was there;
all along the Way.

# way
# to go

## part 2

## Extending the invitation

# day 19

# Move out and multiply

Matthew 28:16–20

'Go and train people all over the world in the same way that I trained you by watching and learning from everything I did and taking note of what I said both publicly and in private.'*

The importance of a mission statement is widely recognized throughout the business world. We need an underlying purpose and goal that determines the activities in which we engage and those in which we don't. There is nothing new in this line of thinking. Centuries ago Jesus brought his ministry to a clear focus in the Great Commission that he gave his followers.

The meeting place he arranged with his followers is both significant and surprising – Matthew's Gospel was written primarily for a Jewish audience, which would lead us to assume that it would end where Mark and Luke conclude their accounts, with Jesus in Jerusalem. Why does Jesus arrange to meet with his disciples in the north of the country, remote from the scene of his crucifixion? There are two possible reasons.

The first is that most of his followers were located in Galilee rather than in Judea and it is likely that, in addition to the eleven specifically mentioned by Matthew, more than 500 gathered to overhear what Jesus had to say. This would seem to be the occasion Paul had in mind in 1 Corinthians 15:6, and would explain the presence of those who 'doubted' in the sense that they were not yet ready to worship Jesus as Lord. Such a large gathering would have been politically impossible under the noses of the Jewish and Roman authorities in Jerusalem.

The second reason is that Galilee was known as 'Galilee of the nations' because it was the territory through which merchants and armies moved when travelling from the east to Egypt and North Africa. What more appropriate place to give his charge to go to the nations?

Jesus encourages the worshippers as well as reassuring the doubters with his opening words: *'All authority in heaven and on earth has been given to me'* for he had completed the mission his heavenly Father had entrusted to him. They needed to know that there was no place they could be sent where he was not already present and that he was in ultimate control of events. Consequently his followers could boldly go where he had gone before. Jesus is now seated at his Father's right hand. His mission was about to become their mission just as he had promised. There is a chain of command – *'As the Father has sent me, I am sending you'* (John 20:21). We only dare venture into the world because he now reigns over the world.

When we talk about sharing the good news our emphasis is most frequently on inviting people into a welcoming church, and for the church to be seeker-sensitive. By contrast, the emphasis in the Great Commission is on our going into the world. As you will have noticed in all of the encounters we have considered so far, Jesus is constantly on the move, meeting people as he journeys from place to place.

Throughout the New Testament we find this constant movement. First and foremost the church signifies people on the move rather than an edifice with a fixed address. We congregate for worship, training and fellowship, but then we disperse in mission reinvigorated by our time together. Therefore, at the end of a church service a congregation is never *dismissed*, but always *dispersed*.

The church goes with a clear sense of purpose. It disperses into the world with the goal of inviting other people to join them in following Christ and that invitation is extended to people of all walks of life and of every race. His closest followers know precisely what Jesus is talking about because they themselves had been through the experience. Only when we ourselves are following Christ are we in a position to invite others to accompany us. In other words, it takes a disciple to make a disciple. His followers in every age are expected to continue his training model.

A follower of Jesus is someone who has received God's forgiveness, and has left behind their old manner of life, in order to risk everything in identifying with Christ and joining the company of those committed to him. Baptism signifies both the need for cleansing and burial and resurrection. We also acknowledge that God had his hand on us before we yielded our life to him. It was the Father who planned our rescue and freedom to live a new life. It was the Son who implemented that plan by coming among us and dying for us; and that it was the Holy Spirit who applied that plan to our lives, and who works within us to make it a reality.

When we think of baptism in those terms we realize that it is a big deal. For the first-century believers it was a costly step that might put one's life on the line. **If you have been baptized, what does it mean to you now?**

Teaching in Christ's academy is not restricted to a short course of instruction, nor is there a graduation ceremony after a few years of study. It is a school for life-long learning. The graduation ceremony does not take place until after death. There's an old saying that states, 'You haven't taught anything until somebody has learned something.' Jesus goes one step further.

We haven't learned something until we have done something about it! In Christ's academy the goal is not simply head knowledge but character formation, ministry involvement and mission engagement. And we don't have the luxury of being selective. We are required to take every course; there are no electives. Becoming a Christ-follower means paying close attention to all that he taught, and in helping each other to take appropriate action both individually and corporately. It also means that we will be inviting others to join us, for, as we saw on day 3, the invitation is both to 'follow' and to 'fish'. The one activity leads to the other. We should not separate what God has linked together.

On days 21 to 25 we will spend some time reviewing and responding to Jesus' teaching to his followers on what a life commitment to him entails. Matthew conveniently brings together a powerful summary in the Sermon on the Mount (chapters 5 – 7). It is only as we understand and apply Jesus' teaching to our own lives that we will be able to communicate that way of living to others.

I expect that you feel as inadequate as I do in responding to such a challenge. But those followers who heard it for the first time must have felt much the same. In all probability they felt even more overwhelmed. It is helpful to know that the Lord has all authority in heaven, but when the crunch comes, heaven can sometimes seem pretty remote.

So the Lord concludes his commission by reassuring them of the intimate nature of his presence: *'And surely I am with you always, to the very end of the age.'* Notice that he does not say 'until the end of their lifetime', rather, his words mean 'throughout the course of human history'. He is as close to us now as he was to them on that occasion. In reality he is even closer. But we will be reassured of his presence to strengthen, protect and guide us only to the extent that we are obedient in response to go and do as he has commanded.

**How far would you go?**
How far would you go to search for God?
To the ends of the earth
and back again?
Beyond your search for all other things?
For health, wealth or happiness?

How far would you go to follow Jesus?
To the ends of the earth
and back again?
Beyond your dedication to any other person?
To your football team, pop idol, or favourite Christian personality?

How far would you go to obey Jesus?
To the ends of the earth
and back again?
Beyond your comfort zone?
To those who are hungry, thirsty, in prison?

Jesus went all the way to the Cross.
Look where that got him, they said.
It got him all the way to us.

day 20

# Back on track

Mark 14:66–72; Acts 2:14–36

> '"I tell you, I do not know the man ..."
> Peter stepped forward and shouted to the
> crowd: "People of Israel, God has made this
> Jesus, whom you crucified, both Lord and
> Christ."'*

Many people go through life emotionally crippled as a result of some
failure in their life from which they have never recovered. Their self-
confidence has been shattered. They feel rejected and permanently
disqualified. The apostle Peter could so easily have become such a
victim, were it not for the restoring power of God's love and the
strength given to him by the gift of the Holy Spirit.

Impetuous people are especially vulnerable to suffer in this way.
Peter was prone to speak and act first, only to have to swallow his
words and live with the unanticipated consequences of his actions.
At Caesarea Philippi, he was the spokesperson for the disciples in
declaring Jesus to be the Messiah. Jesus had asked who the crowds

considered him to be. What was the word on the street? They told him most people thought he was the prophet sent to prepare for the coming of the Lord. Then, he had asked the disciples directly, *'But what about you? . . . Who do you say I am?'* Peter had given the right answer, yet he closes his ears to Jesus' warnings that he must undergo great suffering, and be rejected by the leaders of Israel (Mark 8:31). Peter had his own ideas as to the place the Messiah would hold and what he would accomplish for his people, and that wasn't part of the picture. So he took Jesus aside to try and dissuade him from upsetting everybody by saying such things.

Sometimes the most ardent supporter can present the greatest obstacle. Jesus gets Peter's attention by commanding him, *'Get away from me, Satan! You are seeing things merely from a human point of view, not from God's'* (v. 33, New Living Bible). Jesus speaks sharply, knowing that his disciples had now to face the fact of his rejection and crucifixion. So he repeatedly comes back to the issue. They were demonstrating that 'there is none so deaf as those who don't want to hear'. It was this denial that made them all the more vulnerable.

On the night of Jesus' betrayal, after the meal that was to be their last supper together, they made their way to the Mount of Olives singing as they went. But Jesus knew that these worshippers would soon turn into deserters. He faces them with the fact that they would be on the run within a few hours: *'[God] will strike the shepherd, and the sheep will be scattered'* (Mark 14:27). True to character, Peter immediately protests that even if everyone else deserted, he would be the exception: *'I will not,'* he claims.

Just like Peter, we are not as strong as we think we are. Surrounded by the right people, we declare our unswerving loyalty. But in other, less welcoming company we present a very different image. Accusations and taunts can cause us to wither.

Jesus, always a true judge of character, had given Simon a new name: 'Peter', the Rock. He was to become the rock in both senses of that word. At times he displayed a firm, rock-like faith, whereas at other times he rocked unsteadily. His new name reflected what Jesus would help him to become, but the road ahead would be a bumpy one.

Yet again, Jesus gives him a blunt warning, telling him '... *today – yes, tonight – before the cock crows twice you yourself will disown me three times.'* Once again Peter is not prepared to listen. That he should deny Jesus was unthinkable, and the other disciples joined his protest.

But, of course, Jesus was proved right. They were all at a low ebb emotionally and physically. While Jesus is uttering his agonizing prayer in the Garden of Gethsemane, his disciples are asleep and unable to overcome their exhaustion. That is until they are rudely awakened by the sudden arrival of an armed mob, led by one of their own number, Judas, who had come to betray Jesus to the authorities.

They were totally unprepared, and ran for their lives. But Peter follows at a safe distance to see Jesus brought to trial before the council in the house of the high priest. His presence does not go unnoticed. He is challenged, not by one of the priests or a Roman soldier, but by a servant girl: *'You also were with that Nazarene, Jesus.'* Twice he denies his association with Jesus and then the cock crows three times. And that familiar sound could have crippled him for life. Every morning from that day forward when he heard the dawn announced by the rooster, Jesus' words could have haunted him.

The vital lesson that Peter had to learn, and that many of his subsequent followers have to recognize, is that failure need not be final. Rather it is a time of self-awareness, when we come to realize that we can follow Jesus only by listening attentively to all that he teaches, and especially to those things we do not want to hear. Those are probably the truths we need the most. Peter broke down and cried. He was down but not out. He did not drown in his tears.

Let's fast-forward through the next few weeks. Jesus is crucified. Then the disciples in Jerusalem begin to hear reports, which they personally verify, that the tomb where he was laid was empty. The stone was rolled away, and Jesus had appeared to some of their number alive. During the next forty days, he meets with them on several occasions, suddenly and without warning. Then he tells them that they are all to gather in Galilee, where they receive their instructions and are commissioned to carry on his mission, going throughout the world to invite people to join them as disciples of Jesus. But first they are to return to Jerusalem for a farewell meeting and to witness Jesus' ascension into heaven. Yet it would not be a farewell – simply a change of relationship.

In Jerusalem they await the long-promised gift from their heavenly Father; his Holy Spirit, who would empower them for mission. As promised, he comes to transform the frightened disciples into bold witnesses. They leave the safety of their room to declare God's words of power in the many languages spoken by the crowds gathered there from around the Mediterranean to celebrate the beginning of harvest. Why would God inspire his witnesses to use the languages of the people these pious Jews had left behind on pilgrimage? The message of the good news about Jesus was intended to reach to the ends of the earth.

When the crowds demand an explanation, it is Peter, the very one who had denied his Lord before a servant girl and a fireside group of nobodies, who now stands before this great crowd. He is now the spokesperson for the apostles and other disciples who had been at that life-changing prayer meeting. And with no time for preparation he has to give unswerving testimony and preach his first sermon. And what a sermon it was! Before he began to speak, the crowd was asking, *'What does this mean?'* By the end, they were demanding, *'What shall we do?'* And Peter tells them the steps they need to take in order to follow Jesus as their Saviour and Lord. From that time on there was no turning back.

**On denial**
I can't deny it:
there are times I have failed you miserably.
I can't deny it:
there are times I've disowned you.
I can't deny it:
I might even do it again.
I can't deny it:
I was a fool to ever let you down.

I can't deny it:
what we had was so real and so good that it was the best thing on
  earth.
I can't deny it:
half the time I don't know what I've got till it's gone.
I can't deny it:
you make me complete.
I can't deny it:
you're all I ever wanted.
I can't deny it:
I've screwed up again.
I can't deny it:
I want you back.
I can't deny it:
I'm so grateful for forgiveness.
I can't deny it:
your love is extraordinary and contagious.
I can't deny it:
in fact, I don't know how I ever did.
I can't deny it:
I love you.
I can't deny it:
I want the whole damn world to know.

I can't deny it:
I can't deny it:
I can't deny it:
any longer.

# A life worth living

Matthew 5:1–12

> There is nothing to compare with living
> God's future now and in learning to become
> what God intended us to be.

It takes a disciple to make a disciple. Following Christ involves inviting others to join us in the adventure. Therefore, it should not surprise us that early in his ministry Jesus gathered the disciples – those leaders-in-training – to give them an overview of what discipleship entailed. He did not instruct them in some retreat hideaway but with an audience overhearing the lesson – because that wider audience comprised some of the future learners in Christ's apprentice school.

The fact that Jesus walked up a mountainside with his followers trailing behind him is also significant. Three times in Matthew's Gospel a mountain becomes the site of a significant stage in his ministry. The second occasion was when Jesus took Peter, James and John up a high mountain where Jesus was enveloped for a brief time in heaven's glory and Moses and Elijah appeared. They represent the witness to Christ of the law and the prophets. They heard the reassuring voice from heaven, *'This is my Son, whom I love; with him I am well pleased. Listen to him!'* (Matthew 17:5). The third occasion is on the mountain in Galilee where they were commissioned for their worldwide task of making disciples.

We will be thinking about the first occasion during the next five days. Here, Jesus gives a major summary of his teaching on discipleship. Some scholars have compared the occasion with Moses giving the law on Mount Sinai. But, as we will see, the good news brought by Jesus results in a very different kind of 'law'.

Jesus' first word to his disciples is a word of encouragement and affirmation. The word he uses nine times is notoriously difficult to translate into modern English. It is usually translated *'blessed'*, which sounds rather benign and churchy to our ears. Other suggestions to bring out the meaning are: 'fortunate are ...', or 'it will go well with ...', or even 'congratulations!' Having been a frequent visitor to Australia, and now having a couple of Australians I see regularly at Fuller Seminary, where I work, I think I would translate it, 'Good-on-ya!'

Whatever word or phrase we use, it is evident that the term is far from benign when you see just who are 'blessed' in specific areas of life. It is important that these nine beatitudes be treated together like a bunch of bananas, rather than considered in isolation. When we bring these descriptions together to build a composite picture they form a character portrait of Jesus himself.

As we begin the journey of faith we need to recognize that this journey is not for down-in-the-mouth losers. God's first word to us is not to draw attention to our shortcomings, or pour guilt on us – but to welcome us with a hearty 'Good-on-ya!' But when we learn just who Jesus considers to be the fortunate ones, then we find ourselves in an upside-down kind of world. As we travel along with Jesus and his followers nothing looks like it once did.

Here are the nine markers that indicate who is truly fortunate:

• The fortunate individuals are those who are have come to end of their own resources and have learned to depend on God. They are no longer self-satisfied, standing on their rights or attempting to justify themselves. They have handed their lives over to God so that he can express his love and purposes through them. That's what it means to live within the sphere in which God rules. God's kingdom values and resources are available now, not on the far side of the rainbow.

• The fortunate individuals are those who see themselves as they really are and see the world around them with its insoluble problems – and they grieve over that. In so doing we will know the heart of God: his depth of concern, his patience, his ultimate purpose for the world he came to save. Such a realization will provide us with a sense of well-being that can come from no other source. Because only God can forgive and make new, and he wants to begin to do that through his apprentices – you and I.

• The fortunate individuals are those who are considerate towards others and who are not always trying to be one better than everyone else. To be meek does not mean to be cowardly, avoiding confrontation at any cost. On the contrary it means being gentle, controlled and yet firm. It means rejecting the 'me-first' competitive assertiveness of our culture, and demonstrating a more caring society based on consideration of other people. Meekness is not underestimating yourself but forgetting yourself. In the long run it is such people who have the greater influence, for it demonstrates the societal value of treating others in the same way that we would like them to treat us.

• The fortunate individuals are those who are passionately concerned for a more just society. We need to remember that the audience on the mountainside largely consisted of people who were poor by this world's standards, had suffered the loss of property, land and those whom they held dear. They knew what it was like to scrape out an existence in face of the unreasonable and sometimes unbearable demands placed upon them by greedy landowners, grab-all tax-collectors, condemnatory religious leaders and a capricious army of occupation. However, satisfaction does not come from taking revenge, but from pursuing a right relationship with God. As in many politically tense regions today, it was all too easy to trigger a spiral of violence. Jesus was well aware of revolutionary groups that were planning an armed insurrection with disastrous consequences.

• The fortunate individuals are those who are forgiving towards other people, understanding the pressures they are under, recognizing the influences that have fuelled their prejudices and hostility, seeking to help them to have a better attitude and to improve their performance. When we remember the mistakes we have made and the people who believed in us and were prepared to give us a fresh start, then we will be less judgmental towards other people. Consideration and forgiveness are contagious and create a positive climate. As followers of Jesus we are in the people-building business.

• The fortunate individuals are those who have cleaned out their lives, determining to become what God intended. As we refuse to tolerate the contradictions in our lives and learn to live more consistently, so we will see God more clearly. We must renounce self-seeking hidden agendas and become transparent. What you see is what you get! Jesus' closest followers could say of him that he was full of grace and truth. In other words, he was both considerate and generous in the extreme as well as being genuine through and through. It is as we become more like Jesus that we see God's true nature more and more clearly.

• The fortunate individuals are those who are the reconcilers and peacemakers. This comes as a special challenge to followers who become increasingly contentious and confrontational, on the mistaken assumption that God has called them to be a judge, jury and jailer instead of a witness. Peacemaking requires the ability to help people calm down, and to listen patiently and actively to one another. A true peacemaker works for the well-being of all and is skilled at transforming situations for the better.

• The fortunate individuals are those who have learned how to face opposition. Jesus is not speaking theoretically for there is already mounting opposition which will lead to attacks against his person. And when the author of this Gospel wrote these words, the communities he was writing for were themselves suffering rejection by society. Some people bring hostility upon themselves because of their unwise words and inappropriate actions. Some protests may have more to do with personal quirkiness, political ambition or simple attention-seeking. The persecution Jesus has in mind is the hostility of the world towards people who, in the opening words, have learned to face opposition. Darkness finds it impossible to coexist with light. Conflict is inevitable, yet the fortunate individual is the person who has developed the right response to put-downs and false-accusations. We can rejoice and be glad that we have not been sucked into their dark and destructive world, but that heaven is both our present experience and future reward.

Every blessing presents a challenge. As we review these nine markers that indicate a true follower of Jesus, they present a formidable obstacle course. But as we hear the starter's gun, we hear Jesus say, 'With my help you can do it – good-on-ya!' And he is already at the finishing tape waiting to shout 'Congratulations!'

**Which of these markers is the Holy Spirit nudging you to work on most urgently? How will you respond?**

### Profit and loss

I would like to make a profit out of loss,
to understand the true nature of being rich.

I would like to see weakness as real strength,
to disarm evil not by force but by love.

I would like to grieve with those who have no one else to turn to,
and cry with those whose tears speak louder than words.

I would like to put the fear of God into those who are tough
by making myself vulnerable instead of standing up for myself.

I would like to find myself by finding God,
and become more fully me by being transformed into his likeness.

I would like to stand up and stand out for peace,
because I live in a peaceful land and want others to know what it's
    like.

And I would like to stay as pure as I can within a dirty world,
not to be holier than the rest, but to see God, through my life, touch
    others.

day 22

# Getting to the
# heart of the matter

Matthew 5:13–48

> 'I am calling you to go beyond what you
> already think you know, so that you will
> bring out the true flavour I intended life to
> have and become lights of hope in a dark
> and depressing world.'*

One of the obstacles we have to overcome in beginning the journey
of faith is the phoney versions of Christianity to which many of
us have been exposed or which we thought might have been the
genuine article. Today's portion of Jesus' Sermon on the Mount pulls
away the religious substitutes that have camouflaged the real thing
for so long that we had little idea what was underneath. Two
common characteristics of phoney faith are uselessness and abusiveness. Let's put our faith to these tests.

First, phoney faith serves no useful purpose in society. More precisely, it is conspicuous by its absence. It is safely contained like salt in a salt-pot or concealed like light under a bucket. Faith can do good only if it is released on society. This may be unobtrusive, like salt shaken over a meal adds flavour. Or it may be there for all to see, like lights from a city on a hill-top, or as a solitary light placed on a stand to brighten a room. But the problem is not simply a matter of the salt being confined. With phoney faith the salt has been adulterated. Outward appearances can be deceptive. The white stuff looks like salt but certainly doesn't taste like it. An even greater contradiction is light that has no impact on the darkness around.

The notions of 'tasteless salt' and 'dark light' are oxymorons. They simply do not make sense. We are not talking here about sub-standard discipleship, but about phoney discipleship that needs to be exposed for what it is.

Once we become the real thing and penetrate like salt and light we begin to impact society. We will then discover that a little can go a long way. When authentic followers of Jesus are released on the world they can make an impact far greater than their numerical strength. In likening his followers to salt and light Jesus is referring to what we are and not simply what we do. But at the same time our profession of faith needs to be validated by deeds that are motivated by God's love. This way we demonstrate that heaven is closer than we think.

We now turn to the second give-away characteristic of phoney faith, which is abusiveness. All too often in the course of history religion has been used as a means of control. This is true at the national and tribal level and within the church and family. In the examples that Jesus gives he switches the emphasis from outward constraints and conformity to inner motivation and a deeper fulfilment of the intention of the law. While good laws can help protect the weak and restrain evil, they have their limitations. You cannot legislate morality. Laws can deal only with antisocial acts and words but have no power to change the demeaning and destructive thoughts that have given rise to them.

Jesus sets his teaching alongside the law of Moses that was the basis of personal and social ethics in Israel. He begins by making it clear that he has not come to set all that aside. He is neither destroying nor editing the statute book as if some of its requirements are too trivial to be followed. His teaching does not deny the law but fulfils it. The law must stand until the love of God has unrestricted access to human hearts. The reign of Christ on earth is not one in which everyone is free to do as they like, claiming that God has made them that way, or that God has told them that what they do is OK. God's revealed word and God's Spirit must not be set in opposition. Jesus cautions his followers against taking any notice of so-called teachers who pursue this line of reasoning. Such teachers can be heard in our own day. The good news of Jesus is not religion-lite, but a radicalized faith of religion-light.

Jesus must have stunned his audience when he declared to them, *'Unless your righteousness surpasses that of the Pharisees and the teachers of the law, you will certainly not enter the kingdom of heaven.'* If these morality police who monitored the religious observance of the nation were not making the grade, what hope was there for the rest of society? The point that Jesus is getting across is that rigorous legalism provides no hope of getting right with God, which is why he came to bring a different kind of righteousness. The righteousness he taught was that which flowed from a right relation-ship with God. It was not something that we accumulate to earn God's favour on a point system; rather, it is the fruit of a life submitted to God. He is not talking of more of the same, but of a superior kind of righteousness. He now illustrates what this means in practical terms.

First, consider the case of *murder*. The law is clear that this is a capital offence and must be judged accordingly. But Jesus is concerned with the attitudes that give rise to the desire to kill, whether or not the person has the opportunity or the determination to carry out their intention. If looks could kill, then the homicide rate would escalate beyond control. Elsewhere Jesus taught that our evil actions arise out of a wicked heart. Not only murder but anger places us under the judgment of God. Resentment, jealousy and contempt all come into this category. Who then can justify a plea of 'not guilty' in response to Jesus' interpretation of the law? Keeping this law means showing respect towards every person, asking for forgiveness and seeking reconciliation at the earliest possible moment. From curbing extremes of behaviour, we have to move to building a courteous, respectful and forgiving climate in society.

Second, consider the case of *adultery*. Cheating on one's spouse has a long history, only today it has less of a public stigma, and in some circles it is even regarded as a means to reinvigorate a jaded relationship! Part of the reason for the more casual attitudes prevalent today is that we have confused love and lust. It is assumed that there is no harm in looking, even to the extent of indulging erotic fantasies. But Jesus challenges this. For once the heart has become obsessed, the act becomes almost inevitable once the opportunity presents itself. That opportunity can be imposed by sexual harassment or enticed by sexual advancement.

Third, consider the case of *divorce*. As in our own day this was widespread and caused a great deal of anguish and havoc in the lives of the vulnerable party. And therein lies the difference between then and now, for then the vulnerable party was always the wife. Husbands took advantage of the exceptions made in the law to divorce their wives for the most trivial of reasons. They could remarry with relative ease, whereas the spouse was regarded as 'soiled goods'. Her hopes of remarriage were slight, and that meant that she could not afford to be too choosy when it came to any subsequent offers. If her family did not take her in to provide support and protection, then she was often reduced to prostitution.

Jesus is concerned to uphold the marriage relationship, for divorce is always damaging to both parties. In some instances it is the better of two sad alternatives, especially in cases of spousal cruelty and cynical habitual infidelity. While adultery may be a justifiable reason for divorce, it does not demand that such action be taken. Repentance and counselling might still rescue the damaged relationship. The marriage relationship is more than a social contract to be maintained only as long as both parties are in agreement, but a solemn covenant in which each person pledges himself or herself to his or her spouse through the changing circumstances of life. It may take a lifetime to develop compatibility!

Fourth, the case of *oath taking.* In a God-fearing society invoking God's name is a serious matter. Various devices were employed to distinguish those oaths you really meant from those you didn't. We played a childhood version of this game: when declaring 'scout's honour' it counted if, at the same time, you made the scout's salute with three fingers, but it didn't if you only saluted with two fingers! The underlying concern here is being untrustworthy and devious. Challenging such devices, Jesus calls us always to say what we mean, and to deliver on our promises.

Fifth, the case of *retaliation.* When the law required *'Eye for eye, and tooth for tooth'*, this was with the intention of curbing revenge-taking and stemming the escalation of violence through vendettas. It was not demanding that like be repaid with like. Jesus takes matters a stage further by counselling that it is better to resist the temptation to strike back. By not doing the expected thing, we unbalance our assailant. But Jesus is not saying we should cave in to violence. Notice the first blow is to the right cheek, which when delivered by a right-handed person means not a punch but a slap with the back of the hand. Jesus is saying how we should respond to an insult intended to demean, not a punch designed to put someone on their back. In such an incident, we turn the other cheek in order to gain the moral advantage, and make our assailant look foolish.

Similarly, in the case of the soldier demanding that a stranger carry his heavy pack – the person has no choice but to obey the command. But their offer to carry the pack a second mile is their own free choice. Try miming each of these incidents and their amusing side will become apparent.

Sixth, the case of *loving your enemies.* The requirement of the law to love one's neighbour was applied in a very restrictive and discriminatory way. Your neighbour was whom you chose. The implication was that you have to love only your neighbour and are at liberty to hate your enemy. The issue is not whom must I treat as a neighbour, but whom can I welcome as my neighbour. The circle of love does not consist of an exclusionary, inward-facing huddle, but of an outward-facing, welcoming circle.

We are prepared to love those who want nothing to do with us. We include the youngest, oldest, strangest, weakest and those we find most difficult to get along with.

Confess before God any of these teachings of Jesus' that prick your conscience today.

As with the nine markers that we considered yesterday, distinguishing those whom God favours, these six characteristics of genuine faith must be taken together. To be perfect does not mean to be without blemish. But we can be made whole because our response to God is both whole-hearted and comprehensive. We are no longer living a double life. It means connecting the dots so that a clear picture emerges of God in action in every area of our life.

### Open Heart

As you read this meditation, feel your pulse, and think about what drives you, what makes you tick. What gets you up in the morning? What are the desires of your heart?

If they could examine a heart for its true content,
what would yours contain?
If they could take an X-ray that saw right through
the flesh and bones, to way beyond all the excuses,
the pretence, the appearances of respectability ...
to the very heart of the matter,
to the attitudes,
the reactions,
the prejudices,
the instincts,
the accumulation of the incidents and happenings
of a lifetime's relationships?

If they could take a stethoscope and listen out
for the beat of your heart,
could they detect the pulse of love,
or monitor life – real life – coursing through your veins?

I know that I am sick, and need God
to help me love.
I would like open heart surgery;
for I would like an open heart.
Without it, I may not live;
at least, not to the full.

And that, I now appreciate,
is my heart's desire.

# What are we like when no-one is looking?

Matthew 6:1–18

> Don't practise your religion in order to impress other people. Make sure that there is more happening behind the scenes than in the public eye.

It is clear from yesterday's reflections that Jesus places great emphasis on character. Character-building is the foundation for appropriate and consistent public conduct. Yesterday we saw how Jesus was concerned not only with inappropriate actions, but with the attitudes they lay behind them. Today we see how he attacks ostentatious piety by looking behind the masks that people wear to reveal what their faith is really like.

Is our religion mostly a show put on to impress other people, or does it have substance? In other words, what are we like when we step off the public stage, when nobody is looking? – except God! Sometimes we are so enamoured with the character we play that we imagine that we are really like that. We forget who we are. This is especially a problem for 'religious professionals' who, like a stage actor, can become intoxicated by their audience and believe their own publicity.

Once again we notice that Jesus' teaching style is not to talk in the abstract, but to use attention-getting illustrations. His verbal pictures are the equivalent of cartoon drawings or of mime exaggerations; as such they need to be visualized as well as heard. To get to the heart of what Jesus is saying we need to activate our imaginations.

Each of the three verbal pictures provides an illustration relating to a vital activity that should characterize every follower of Jesus Christ, namely: giving to people in need, praying to our God in heaven, and self-denial, here expressed in terms of fasting. These are the basic elements of most religions. In relation to each of these Jesus makes the same point. If you do this simply to impress the people around you, then their applause is all you will hear. That's all the reward you will receive. God is not impressed. He's not even in the audience.

By describing this form of religion-for-show as hypocrisy Jesus emphasizes that public piety is not an act we perform. The Greek term *hypocrite* originally referred to actors who commonly wore masks, from which it came to be used in a figurative sense. A true friend and mentor is the person who tells us what the mask we are wearing looks like to them and then helps us remove it. God is more concerned with what we do in private than with how we perform in public. This is not to say that our faith does not find public expression but rather, when it does, it is consistent with who we really are off-stage. Now let us see how this plays out in the three areas that Jesus deals with:

*Giving to the needy.* This should not be done with a fanfare of publicity, or to get your name inscribed as a major donor, or be honoured at a banquet for benefactors. If our motivation is public recognition then that is all the reward we will receive. Jesus tells his followers that their giving should be undertaken in a very different way. They must not draw attention to themselves. Make sure your giving is anonymous, which is difficult when declared charitable donations are tax deductible, as is the case in the USA! The point is that we must not try to gain social prestige or influence out of our giving. Furthermore, we are not to remind ourselves about what we have given in order to inflate our spiritual egos or to believe that this gives us greater influence with God. For God cannot be lobbied on the basis of our campaign contributions! Dallas Willard's paraphrase gives a new slant to Jesus' command not to let our left hand know what our right hand is doing: 'The question is not so much what the hand is doing, but what the heart is thinking while the hand is doing it.'

*Praying to our heavenly Father.* Jesus again teaches by way of drawing contrasts. The way in which his followers pray must be different both from the religious show-offs and the pagan babblers. The former like to be seen when they pray. They turn it into a public performance. Whereas true prayer is honouring God, they, on the other hand, are seeking to divert attention to themselves. Such self-focused praying rises no higher than a lead balloon.

In contrast, Jesus insists that his followers do as much of their praying as possible out of the public eye. The picture he uses is of someone shutting themselves in a closet or storeroom as the only place where you could find privacy in first-century houses, which were small and open-plan. Evidently Jesus did not mean this literally, for there is no evidence in the Gospels of his following his own instructions. But he did seek the solitude of the mountainside or garden, away from the crowds and his closest followers, in order to pour out his heart to God.

If they are to avoid acting like religious show-offs, they are also to ensure that they do not pray like the pagans who shouted loudly in order to gain the attention of distracted and capricious gods. Their kind of praying resembled the bargaining carried out in the market-place. They sought to trade on favours owed. Such prayer was like attempting to draw up a contract with a deity.

Jesus' way of praying was altogether different. And his model is to be ours. First, it is based on a deep relationship that is both intimate and respectful. People who have had inadequate, unfaithful or abusive human fathers may struggle with this way of addressing God. But this is how Jesus taught us to pray, so we must learn from him what a true father is like, and allow our understanding of God as Father to redefine fatherhood for us, rather than allowing our experience to colour our understanding of the father role God intended. This in itself can be deeply healing.

Second, the prayer is corporate rather than confined to the individual. It is the prayer of the community that has become the family of God by adoption. Addressing God in such relational terms is a privilege that we are granted, not a right that we can demand. Pagans cannot pray in such terms. Even in Jewish prayer, God is never directly addressed as 'Father'. It is a family prayer of the community that has responded to Christ's offer of forgiveness and his death and resurrection to reconcile us to his heavenly Father. Through the only Son of God we become adopted sons and daughters.

Third, the prayer begins with the glory of God, not with a catalogue of our needs and requests. It is a self-reminder that God is in heaven, which does not signify his remoteness but his full awareness, sovereign power and accessibility. *'Heaven'* is really plural 'heavens' indicating its far-reaching dimensions. The presence of Jesus makes heaven a close encounter, for with his coming the kingdom of heaven is at hand; not just out of sight over the horizon, but all around us. It is at hand and no longer beyond our reach. This truth is reinforced by the statement, *'hallowed by your name'*. God's name is honoured in the doing of his will. The followers of Jesus represent the character and concerns of God before a watching world. Does our personal and corporate witness serve to honour or bring discredit on God? We may not be able to say with the sinless Son of God, *'Anyone who has seen me has seen the Father'* (John 14:9), but we must pray that those who watch us glimpse something of Jesus. People may not be looking for perfection, but they are looking for authenticity.

Fourth, the prayer is driven by a vision of God's will being done on earth as it is in heaven. We are inspired by the promise of a better world where God has his way. This is not a utopian dream to be achieved through the process of human evolution, but a reality that will come about only through divine intervention. But until that time, the community he has left on earth, and which he intends to extend throughout the earth, is an anticipation of his coming. As such it will always be a pilgrim church in the process of becoming, despite its inner contradictions.

Fifth, the prayer is concerned with our immediate and urgent needs. In fact we must appreciate the urgency in the words of the prayer we have already considered. This is the prayer of desperate people, many of them the oppressed underdogs of Palestinian society. They lived a hand-to-mouth existence and depended on the provision of a heavenly Father even for the barest essentials. Another fact of life was the constant struggle to pay back debts incurred through the crushing burden of taxation. They pleaded with God to forgive them their debts, which was a familiar way of speaking of sins among Jews. But first they had to be willing to forgive other unfortunates around them for the debts they could not hope to pay back, before they could expect the same treatment from God, to whom they owed so much more.

Sixth, they pray that God will give them strength not to cave in under the pressures they face, not to compromise or to wangle deals that will lead them even further into trouble. Sometimes we need to be delivered from ourselves as much as from the evil one, who lurks to exploit any unwise move we make.

With this brief treatment we quickly realize that this is not a prayer that we can rattle-off in twenty seconds flat. It provides both a framework to organize our prayers, and mineshafts to bring increasing depths to our prayer.

*Fasting as an expression of devotion and self-denial.* Among most easy-going and self-indulgent Western Christians fasting is an all-too-rare discipline. I include myself in their number. In contrast, fasting was a commonplace discipline among the devout of the first century, as it is today among Muslims, Hindus and Buddhists. Jesus does not include it as an option. He does not say '*if* you fast' but '*when* you fast'. When people fasted they not only abstained from food for a season, but at the same time spoiled their public image by failing to cut or tidy their hair or wash either themselves or their clothes, and definitely no sex. They turned it into a social statement.

When self-denial is practised by Jesus' followers they are not to make it obvious. On the contrary, they will appear clean and tidy so that nobody will know that they are exercising self-denial to a special degree. Fasting is not a device for twisting God's arm, but rather one way of expressing our dependence upon God's grace and strength.

> What act of love and service to God could you perform quietly today?

**Honest to God**
Honest to God
He's my father.

Honest to God,
I want to see the kingdom come and his will done.

Honest to God,
I forgive those who hurt me.

Honest to God,
I need forgiveness.

Honest to God,
We've a long way to go.

Honest to God,
I need your help.

Honest to God,
I'll try to be the same person to you as I am to me.

Honest to God,
I'm not in it for the kudos.

Honest to God,
I'm honest to God.

Honest to God,
Are you listening?

Honest to God
This is between you and me.

Honest to God,
That's all ...

... For that's enough:
I want to be honest to God.

day 24

# Learn to travel light

Matthew 6:19 – 34

> 'Don't store up your treasure on earth but in heaven ... Don't worry about how you look or how long you will live ... Seek first God's kingdom and his righteousness.'*

Most of us cart about too much clutter with us as we travel through life. Our baggage may be material possessions that weigh us down and hamper our progress, or it may be mental baggage. Our cares and worries can be just as burdensome. If it's not one, it's the other that will get us down, and some people stagger under the double burden. Jesus demands that we learn to off-load our burdens to enjoy the freedom of travelling light. For those of us who habitually pack too much every time we take a journey, just in case, have you noticed how much of the stuff you carried around and never needed anyway?

Yet, we never accumulate enough to satisfy us for very long. Yesterday's luxuries have the habit of turning into today's essentials. My wife and I watched the BBC TV documentary series *Nineteen Hundred House* that traced the fortunes of a modern family living in a house that had been restored to its turn-of-the-century condition, surviving only on the provisions and implements available at the time. They barely made it, and were so relieved to return to their modern choices, comforts and conveniences.

Earth is an insecure place to store our prized possessions and essential belongings. New things don't stay new for very long. Rust spots soon begin to show on the car and clothes develop moth-holes, or simply wear thin after a few sessions in the washing machine. Then, you can never know when the next break-in is coming. The stock market takes a dive. Nothing is safe, no matter how sophisticated a surveillance and alarm system we install. Perhaps it's high time we divested ourselves of some of that worrisome stuff.

We have to ask ourselves what it is we really set our hearts on, and what continually catches our attention. Which shops do we gravitate to each time we walk down the high street? Which advertisements catch our attention when we open a magazine or a newspaper, or turn on the TV? That's what we consider treasure. Treasure is something we hoard rather than use.

Jesus describes the eye as a lamp; in other words, a source of light, that fills the whole body. We then have to ask ourselves what images it is projecting. On what is it focusing attention? A concentration on just one theme, with picture after picture, indicates any obsession that we might have developed. Are those images wholesome or corrupting? Do they fill us with life-generating light or depressive and destructive darkness?

A literal translation of 'good' eye is 'single' eye; that is, we focus on one thing, and in so doing relegate everything else to its proper place as well as eliminate some items altogether. A slave cannot serve two masters when each demands absolute allegiance. If we attempt the impossible we will end up making one of them our enemy. We cannot serve both God and money/possessions. The term

Jesus employed covers both. Craig Keener, in his commentary on this passage, notes that 'its contrast with God as an object of service here suggests that it has been deified as well as personified'. Whatever we allow to take the place of God has become our idol.

**Is there some baggage that you could divest yourself of today?**

We turn now from accumulating and guarding our possessions, to worries as to whether or not we will have sufficient in the future. We fret about whether we will be able to keep a roof over our head, put food on the table, and replace our clothing as it wears out. In response, Jesus calls us to learn some lessons from nature. Birds live from day to day, demonstrating a carefree industry. We must not misinterpret Jesus by concluding that he is advocating laziness and irresponsibility. He is counselling us against worrying, not against working!

There were some people in the early church who adopted that easy-going lifestyle, and traded off the hospitality and generosity of other believers. They defended their lack of activity on the grounds that the Lord was returning very soon so there was no need for them to get entangled in earthly pursuits. The apostle Paul addresses these individuals in Thessalonica with the blunt comment that those who don't work don't deserve to eat. In the Krüger National Park in South Africa I remember see the warning to visitors not to feed the baboons. Once they become dependent on the food handed to them by tourists – a drive-by food outlet in reverse – they become too lazy to fend for themselves.

Moving from food to clothing, Jesus draws attention to the splendour of the desert display of wild flowers. Their appearance is breathtaking. If God can do that for flowers, we should not be preoccupied about what we will hang on our bodies. It is not the clothes that make the person but the person who makes the clothes. Beauty does not lie primarily in adornment. Even Solomon, Israel's most flamboyant king, was no match for the display God can put on in the field or even in the desert. If God is prepared to go that far for flowers that only last for a few days, what will he do for humankind whom he created in his own image?

Worry doesn't make life better. On the contrary it takes all the sparkle out of it. Neither can we prolong our life by worrying about how long we've got left. We are more likely to shorten it. This section of the Sermon on the Mount concludes with two recipes for a contented life. The first is to get our priorities straight by seeking first God's kingdom, which, you will remember, comes at the beginning of the Lord's Prayer. This does not mean focusing on life beyond the grave, but getting involved in what God is doing right now and discerning what he has in mind for us. Jesus sets us the example in that he did only what he saw the Father doing. God's purpose must have priority over our preoccupations.

Second, we are to learn to live a day at a time. Worry only serves to mortgage tomorrow. There is no point in shouldering tomorrow's burdens in addition to carrying today's. That's why we come apart and burn out. If this was important in Jesus' day, it is an even more important lesson to learn in ours because we live in a culture of such chaos and unpredictable change. We cannot plan for a future that is unpredictable. All we can do is to consider alternative scenarios, and leave it in God's hands. Management is more about coping with today than controlling tomorrow.

**Vogue**
What's in fashion
will very soon be
out of fashion.

But it's cool to keep up
because we want to stay in
with the in crowd.

I always want more;
A myriad choices mean
I'll never be fully satisfied.

And to get more,
I need to concern myself
about tomorrow.

Speculate to accumulate,
feather the nest, even if it's
at the expense of the losers.

I've always wondered
what I would rescue from
my house if it was burning down.

What possession defines
the me of me,
the you of you?

What could I leave behind?
And what could I not afford
to lose?

How would you feel if
You lost all you had? Every last thing.
Naked? Bereft? Not quite yourself anymore?

And the more we have,
the harder it is to say goodbye
to anything. Why is that?

I want to be more than just the
sum of my parts. I want to be

part of you.

# Building to last

Matthew 7

> 'Jesus said, "Everyone who hears these words of mine and puts them into practice is like a wise man who builds his house upon a rock-firm foundation."' *

Drawing contrasts is a most effective teaching device. The alternatives presented leave clear impressions on the mind, identifying the differences of which we need to be aware and the choices we have to make. It is in the daily process of decision-making that we build our lives. The followers of Jesus are provided with guidelines to help in decision making, not given a rulebook that makes the decisions for us. Throughout Matthew 7 we are presented with alternative pictures:

- a person with a plank in his eye and another one with a tiny splinter (another cartoon drawing or mime act)
- gifts of bread or a stone, and of a fish or a snake
- a highway or a footpath, a turnstile or a highway toll-booth

- sheep and wolves
- trees bearing good fruit and trees bearing bad fruit
- wise and foolish builders and a tottering house without foundations as compared with a house built on bedrock.

Jesus knew how to capture the attention of his audience. Such vivid pictures create lasting images.

The first contrast is concerned with judging other people. Most of us are better at seeing the mistakes of other people than addressing our own. If we haven't first dealt with our own issues before endeavouring to correct another person's, we will be as useless and dangerous as a blindfolded surgeon. Perfectionists tend to take themselves too seriously, so Jesus presents them with a ludicrous picture. When people are made to laugh at themselves heartily they will begin to look at themselves honestly. It is less painful to us to remove irritating specks in other peoples' eyes than have to deal with something grotesquely large in our own.

The person we are determined to help will understandably keep out of reach in order to avoid the damage they anticipate we will do if they let us any nearer. The hypocrite plays a dangerous game. What we are trying to do is totally inappropriate. We are acting out of our own needs, not that of the person we are purporting to help. That seems to be the significance of the next word-picture Jesus employs when he says, *'Do not give dogs what is sacred; do not throw your pearls to pigs.'*

The person who is always trying to put other people right does so from an assumed position of moral superiority. When we act in that way, we should not be surprised when our pearls of wisdom are trodden under foot by the people we are attempting to help, and they respond not with a smile of gratitude but with snarls of resentment and even physical retaliation. By contrast, followers of Jesus are those who come alongside to help others by acknowledging that they have had to deal with the same issues in their own lives.

No sooner do we sign up as a follower of Jesus than we realize that our journey involves a daily struggle between the vision that inspires us and the reality that frustrates us. We go through this life as seekers seeking first the kingdom of God. It is this dedicated searching that makes us ask, seek and knock with daily urgency and persistence. As we see signs of God's reign amongst us we want even more evidence of his presence and influence. This is the tension between the 'now' and the 'not yet' of the kingdom. Jesus issues a challenge to persistence together with the assurance that we will prevail. But as Dallas Willard has remarked, the promise that the door will be opened is not an 'open sesame' to satisfy our greed and fantasies. It is God's response to our requests that are in line with his purposes for us.

So if we find that God has not met our demands, we should not feel hard-done-by or that God has responded in a harmful way. God's gifts must not be considered in the same categories as stones and snakes. A loving father neither disregards nor harms his children. He gives good gifts that will bring benefit as well as delight. We in turn need to be as generous in our dealings with other people.

The journey of faith entails walking a narrow path, but it's the preferred path. I often advise American tourists visiting Britain to get off the motorway and drive along the country lanes and walk the bridle paths. Popular advice is to 'go with the flow', which in reality may entice us to join the lemmings in their stampede over the cliff. Followers of Christ are more likely to find themselves swimming against the tide.

Not only is the road narrow but the gate of entry is small. You have to leave a lot of baggage on the other side and stoop low to enter. Our clutter and aloofness may disqualify us from starting on the journey, as the rich young ruler discovered whom we encountered on day 14. There were few travellers along the narrow way in the first century because of a combination of factors, including failure to uphold ethical standards, to relinquish material ambitions, and to face persecution.

Another important consideration in building to last is to make sure that we are listening to and learning from the right people. A prophet is a person who claims to speak on behalf of God. In every age there has been no shortage of false prophets who entice people off God's narrow way and onto their own highway or diversionary path. At first sight they might seem harmless; indeed we might mistake them for being one of us from outward appearances. But under the surface they are a different animal – a ferocious wolf. Wolves cannot simply be shooed away. They need a much firmer response.

The next contrast we are faced with is the two kinds of trees. Both bear fruit, but are distinguished by the kind of fruit that they bear and the quality of that fruit. Both trees may be inviting, but on closer inspection we discover that eating from one of the trees will only make us sick because the fruit is bad. For example, we must never let impressive charisma blind us to questionable character. Some people may exercise a spectacular charismatic ministry, with people genuinely healed in Jesus' name, but the teaching associated with that ministry contradicts the teaching of Jesus. God's power at work in an individual's ministry is no guarantee of that person either being in a right relationship with God or their teaching being reliable. Sometimes the Lord chooses to work *through* them *despite* them. The basic building block of discipleship is obedience. It is all too easy to say, *'Lord, Lord'*, but that title is meaningless on our lips if we have not submitted our lives to him.

The last contrast is concerned with two builders. They have both received instructions on how to build, as had the crowd who had listened to Jesus' teaching on the mountainside. The significant difference between the two builders is that one decided to take short cuts and built in the easiest place, whereas the other dug down to bedrock to get a firm foundation. No doubt the first builder was finished first because he had less to do. During fine weather there was no detectable difference between the two houses. However, when the hurricane hit, the impact on those structures was immediately apparent. The house built on the sand fell with a great crash because its sandy base had been washed away. Before long the hurricane of persecution would hit the church, and a flood of new challenges would sweep over it as the followers of Christ took the gospel to non-Jews throughout the Graeco-Roman world.

On this dramatic note Jesus comes to the end of his address to his disciples and his wider audience. The crowds were amazed at his teaching, not so much because it was so graphic and interesting (though it was), but because he taught with the authority of someone who lived out his teaching and who did not need to quote the scholars to buttress what he said. He was his own authority. We are not told of the response of his close followers. Perhaps their reaction was not so much amazement as of being overwhelmed. You can never reduce Jesus' teaching to snack-size portions – it is always more food than we can manage, and is a feast to which we have to return repeatedly.

> Remember significant life decisions you have made, and acknowledge the hand of God in either affirming or overriding them.

## Now and not yet

Instant solution,
Instant karma.
Quick fit,
Quick fix.
Buy now.
Pay later!
I want it all,
and I want it now.

Not yet.

Fast food,
Fast car.
Speedy connection,
Speedier download.
Eat now,
Diet later!
I want it all,
and I want it now.

Not yet.

Beneath the surface of a culture
Stuck on fast forward
Lies depth.
We can skim the surface,
or we can swim deep.

We can speed along the motorway
And go, go, go with the flow.
Or slow down,
Take the scenic route,
Put the brakes on. Stop. Look. Listen.

Now. But not yet.
Can you feel the tension?
Take up the strain.
Go against the flow.
Swim against the tide.

Building to last.

# way
# to go

## part 3

# Lessons along
# the way

# Empowered
# for mission

Acts 2:1–21

> ' "We hear them declaring the wonders of God in our own tongues!" Amazed and perplexed they asked one another, "What does this mean?" '

Guilt is a very poor motivator. We cannot be cajoled into living a life that bears constant witness to its Lord. And our enthusiasm is so often short-lived, being subject, as it is, to the mood of the moment. Jesus employed neither scolding nor motivational talks to prepare his people to continue his work on earth. Rather he told them to wait for the promise of the Father (Luke 24:49; Acts 1:4), which he had spoken about to his disciples both in the upper room just prior to his crucifixion and after his resurrection.

In John's Gospel we read the account of Jesus promising to send another Counsellor, which is translated as Comforter in the older versions. This Comforter will continue the ministry that Jesus had among them but in a more intimate and more extensive manner. The Comforter is the Holy Spirit, who comes, not to make us comfortable but to turn us into witnesses, by opening our mouths and moving us out into the world. This is the special emphasis of Luke.

**What motivates you in your Christian life – is it Jesus-centred and Spirit-powered?**

If that is a tough challenge for the Holy Spirit in our day, it was no less so for the followers of Jesus in his day. Despite the fact that they had heard him teach on the subject, they were disoriented and preferred talking to each other, rather than to the world beyond their depleted ranks.

In response Jesus makes it clear that they should be concerned not with what he will do, but with the mission upon which they are about to embark. *'It is not for you to know the times or dates the Father has set by his own authority. But you will receive power when the Holy Spirit comes on you; and you will be my witnesses in Jerusalem, and in all Judea and Samaria, and to the ends of the earth'* (Acts 1:7–8). Immediately following this he is taken up in a cloud of glory as heaven touches the earth. The disciples linger a while, but an angel reassures them that they need wait no longer, for Jesus will return in the same way as they have seen him go. If they persist in standing there they are in for a long wait!

If we are honest with ourselves, most of us would admit that we are also in need of power from God to enable us to witness faithfully to Christ. But we must not overlook the fact that the power of the Holy Spirit flows from our relationship with God. That intimacy is made possible only by means of all that Jesus accomplished through his sacrificial death and his victorious resurrection and ascension to the place of power at his Father's right hand.

It is clear from the conversation between Christ and his followers in the opening chapter of Acts that they still hadn't got the message. They rejoiced that Jesus was alive. Their hopes were restored, but they had returned to their old preconceptions. Their expectations were that Jesus would now establish his kingdom here on earth, freeing their country from their Roman oppressors, bringing spiritual renewal, and giving his closest companions the top jobs. This is what lies behind their question, *'Lord, are you at this time going to restore the kingdom to Israel?'* (Acts 1:6). Would he make a triumphal entry into Jerusalem, as he had on Palm Sunday, only this time with a different outcome? It was not until Jesus' departure into heaven that this mindset would dissolve. No wonder they were rooted to the spot.

But the Lord had left them with a clear command not to leave Jerusalem, but instead to wait for the gift that his Father had promised them. In obedience to his word they returned to the city, some one hundred and twenty in number, to wait prayerfully on God. In so doing they were learning to pray in a new way, adjusting to their relationship to Jesus now enthroned in heaven. They now prayed in his name.

It was in this context that the Spirit eventually came upon them, in their case in the form of a rushing mighty wind and with flames of fire. The Holy Spirit comes in a form that is appropriate to the people involved and to their circumstances. In the case of Jesus, the Spirit came in the form of a gentle dove to bring reassurance and as a symbol of God's covenant love. The disciples needed the Spirit to get them moving and to inspire their speaking. Any fire-fighter knows that wind and fire together make for an unstoppable combination.

On this occasion the Spirit came suddenly, reminding us that we cannot programme the Spirit's operations. The Spirit came power-fully, but never as destructive brute force. The Spirit came upon all present, not confined to a spiritual elite. Theirs was a communal experience, yet the Spirit came individually with a tongue of fire resting on each of them.

Luke provides our only record of the event of Pentecost, and it is he who establishes a direct link between the experience of the church and the prophetic word of Jesus that the Father's promise was soon to be fulfilled. While other writers of the New Testament emphasize the inner work of the Spirit to produce Christ-like character, Luke's emphasis is on the coming of the Spirit to equip the church to continue the mission of Christ. The timing is significant in that Pentecost was the occasion for the celebration of the first-fruits of the wheat harvest, with the promise of much more to come (Exodus 34:22; Numbers 28:26). For the church it signified the beginning of a spiritual harvest, the harvest produced by Jesus' death, as he had foretold: *'I tell you the truth, unless a grain of wheat falls to the ground and dies, it remains only a single seed. But if it dies, it produces many seeds'* (John 12:24). Indeed, the harvest was great. Three thousand were added to the church that day through Peter's sermon in the Jerusalem temple.

Luke also gives emphasis to the gift of tongues given to the disciples that day. This was a gift of foreign languages not previously learned, which enabled them to declare the wonders of God in the languages of the crowd gathered from around the Mediterranean world for the feast. Now it was not necessary for the disciples to communicate with the audience in their own tongues, because, though diverse, they shared a common language – Greek. So the significance of the gift lay in the fact that these Jewish believers in Jesus were praising God in the languages spoken by the people. In other words, their God was no tribal God who addressed his people only in Hebrew, but he was the God of the nations who related to all peoples everywhere.

You and I cannot keep God to ourselves. The good news is so amazing that we cannot selfishly keep it to our own crowd. The wind represents the driving power of God to fill our sails and to give us confidence to sail out of our safe harbours. The fire represents the refining, warming, illuminating, inspiring and welcoming presence of God. Like that newly born church, we must also seek the filling of the Holy Spirit daily – that we might move under his influence and be inspired when to speak and what to say.

**Spirit of Change**
We didn't really know what we
were waiting for. Orders, I guess.
Still in the dark,
waiting on the word from on high,
blindly determined, somehow,
as though the world depended on it.
Waiting for the future
to spark into life, waiting for the wind
of change to blow in our direction
and take us ... God knows where.

Waiting to fan the flame.

They looked like tongues;
slivers of fire the likes of which no one
has ever seen. Eternal flames,
never to be extinguished, a sign,
for the rest of time, that we are not alone.

That you are not alone.

And the funniest thing is, we spoke in new tongues,
– we who were forever lost for words,
tongue-tied, ignorant, inarticulate.
Speaking life and light to those in the
sun-drenched streets who stood in darkness.

It blows my mind to think of it:
Us and God. Spreading the Word.

In the Spirit of Partnership.

## day 27

# Unplanned journeys

Acts 8

'Those who were scattered as a result of the persecution in Jerusalem spread the word wherever they went. Philip went down to a city in Samaria and proclaimed the Christ ... Now an angel of God said to Philip, "Go south to the desert road that goes down from Jerusalem to Gaza."' *

In the early chapters of Acts every significant new phase in the outreach of the followers of Jesus is as a consequence of God's sovereign initiative rather than human planning. Despite the fact that the Lord had given them such clear instructions, they continue to drag their feet. At the heart of the problem is the fact that they are Jews who face formidable social barriers. Inhibited by centuries of exclusivism, they are afraid of losing their place within Jewish society. It is significant that when the break from traditional Judaism eventually came, it was not through any strategic plan by the leaders of the Jerusalem church, but rather through the Greek-speaking Jews who were more at home with Graeco-Roman society.

The Jewish authorities targeted this Greek-speaking section of the church. They probably felt that they were a soft target, and that they could stamp out the 'Followers of the Way', as the disciples were called, by directing their persecution at them. This would avoid making martyrs of Hebrew-speaking followers. Indeed, Stephen became the first martyr, his death marking the beginning of what Luke describes as *'the great persecution'*. This also explains why all except the apostles were scattered throughout Judea and Samaria.

As it turned out, the persecution had the opposite effect than that intended. Instead of silencing the church and stopping its advance, it simply scattered people who were determined to sow the seeds of the gospel throughout Judea and Samaria. This was a case of mission that was being generated on the periphery as a spontaneous activity. More often than not this is how outreach happens.

It's a bit like the spread of graffiti. There is no central body organizing that global phenomenon. If its proliferation was dependent on an organization, there would be only a fraction of what we encounter on walls, buildings and bridges everywhere today. The gospel spreads like graffiti, not like a professional media-driven campaign!

Among these Greek-speaking witnesses is Philip the evangelist. He proclaims Christ in Samaria, and the power of God is so evidently working through him that Simon, the local sorcerer, feels upstaged and his nose put out of joint. The one who had proclaimed himself to be someone great now encountered someone greater. The more signs and wonders he sees being performed by Phillip the more he wants access to the same powers, at any price.

Hearing of the response to Philip's preaching, the apostles in Jerusalem send two of their number, Peter and John, to investigate. They do not take much convincing that this is a genuine work of God. The Samaritans have not only experienced the power of God but have received the word of God, and they now acknowledge Jesus as their Lord and Saviour. They therefore pray that they might receive the Spirit of God in order to live the life of Christ and to serve him faithfully and effectively. Perhaps, in their case, the coming of the Spirit into their lives was delayed so that the Jerusalem leaders could be directly involved, thereby ensuring a cohesion of Jews and Samaritans.

While it was persecution that drove Philip into Samaria, it was an angel that prompted him to go south. He was to leave a populated city wide-open to the gospel, to go to the desert road that went from Jerusalem to Gaza, with no reason for the journey given. God's guidance comes in many forms, sometimes when we are totally unaware of God's hand in events. And even when his will is revealed, it is one step at a time. Rather like a treasure hunt, all you get is the clue to the next location. It also comes unsought by us so perhaps we need to learn to relax a little more and let events take their course. We simply need a discerning ear and an obedient heart.

Once again we are presented with the extraordinary measures that God will take to bring together the earnest seeker after truth and the faithful witness. If you are the earnest seeker like the Ethiopian official on the road to Gaza, then pray that God will bring alongside someone who is able to listen to your questions and give you some reliable and satisfactory answers. If you want to become a more effective witness, then prepare by being a diligent student of God's word, and by being available when God leads you even when you don't understand what he has in mind! Walking by faith often means that we don't have much of an idea about what God is up to.

On reaching the road Philip meets someone who is obviously a person of great importance, judging by his chariot and retinue. On enquiry he discovers that he is in fact the minister of finance of Queen Candace of Ethiopia. The official had made the long journey to Jerusalem, whether on diplomatic business or a spiritual pilgrimage we do not know. If it was the latter, he had not found the answer to his spiritual search in the temple. Philip hears the Ethiopian reading aloud from a scroll that contained part of the prophecy of

Isaiah, which he had probably purchased in Jerusalem. Now he knows why the angel had directed him to this spot. He plucks up sufficient courage to approach the official's chariot, asking the man if he understands what he is reading. He is invited to ride along to continue the conversation.

Philip immediately recognizes the passage from which he is reading and is able to explain that the person described by the prophet as being led like a sheep to the slaughter is in fact Jesus of Nazareth, who was crucified just outside the walls of Jerusalem. He no doubt went on to explain that although Jesus was taken from the earth, he appeared to his disciples after his death on a number of occasions and is now reigning in heaven.

**How would you explain the significance of Isaiah 53 to an earnest seeker today?**

If some contemporary theologians had been explaining the passage, rather than Philip, it is likely that the official would have continued on his way as confused as ever!

Sometimes an encounter with a stranger means you quickly cover a lot of ground while you have time available. So Philip, aware of the openness of the official and of his joy at having the meaning unlocked of the Bible passage he has been puzzling over, explains the next step to begin the journey of following Christ. Spotting water by the roadside, the official seizes the moment. *'Look, here is water. Why shouldn't I be baptised?'* I wonder if Philip was prepared for such an impetuous response? But, without hesitation, he agreed to the government minister's request. They pull over, and both step into the water so that Philip can baptize him.

After that initiation we hear no more about this Ethiopian in Scripture, but the Coptic Church in Egypt claims its origins from his conversion. Likewise, we may never know the outcomes of a one-time encounter. In any case, God has other urgent work for Philip in the towns of Samaria to establish his base of operations in the Roman garrison town of Caesarea. Philip remained there for more than twenty years.

**Spreading out**

We wanted to spread like wild fire,
like seeds on the wind,
taking life to dead lands,
to the world outside our community, our faith,
and so, we thought, our reach.

But how?

You couldn't plan for this type of thing;
draw up a battleplan, design a logo,
declare a decade of evangelism
to let the flame burn brighter. If only.
My brand burnt and hurt like hell.

Treated like shit, some tortured, some killed,
we were hounded out, and
Spread like muck across the earth.
But the ground grew fertile, and
new shoots of green made a break-through.

It was down to partnership:
ordinary people, with
an extraordinary Spirit.
Organic, real, convincing because
they had been convinced.

Spreading out. Contagious.
It's catching. We've caught the fever.

## day 28

# The reluctant visitor

Acts 10:1 – 11:18

> 'Simon, three men are looking for you. So get up and go downstairs. Do not hesitate to go with them, for I have sent them.'

Today's incident is obviously of great significance for Luke, considering how much time he devotes to the story of Peter and Cornelius finding each other. Space was severely rationed in an ancient scroll so the author had to allocate the length of each section of his writing project carefully. We also know the incident is important because we see God working supernaturally at each end of the line of communication, with Cornelius and Peter both being guided by visions. Furthermore, Peter gives a report to the church leaders in Jerusalem, and omits nothing in the retelling of the story.

We begin with Cornelius, a centurion of the Italian regiment who was billeted in Caesarea, which is where Philip the evangelist was based. Although a non-Jew, Cornelius is described as a God-fearer who prayed regularly and gave generously to the poor. If sincerity was the criterion for acceptance before God then he would have qualified. But his spiritual quest continued, and God answered him with a remarkable vision – revealing to him that he was to send representatives to Joppa to seek out a man named Simon, and bring him back. He selects for the mission two servants and a devout soldier whom he can trust to convey his message accurately and with spiritual sensitivity. Yesterday, we considered God bringing together Philip and the Ethiopian seeker. Today, we encounter a second example of God's intervention. Our sharing of the good news is based on the premise that God is always the primary seeker, and that we are simply his agents willing to make ourselves available.

But sometimes we are reluctant messengers. God recognizes that Simon Peter would be unwilling to respond to the messengers from Cornelius, his suspicions aroused that it was some kind of a trap. So God prepares Simon through a vision he receives during an after-dinner siesta.

He dreams of a large sheet filled with animals, reptiles and birds, which he is commanded to kill and eat. He refuses, protesting that he has never eaten anything that was forbidden according to the law. In response the voice declares, 'Do not call anything impure that God has made clean.' And just to emphasize the point, the vision is repeated twice more. Although the Bible describes this as a vision, I am sure that Simon Peter would have considered it a nightmare.

By now Simon Peter is wide awake and puzzling over the significance of the vision, when the voice from heaven reveals to him to go downstairs where he will find three men looking for him. When they ask him to accompany them to Caesarea to meet their master Cornelius, he is not to hesitate. Sure enough he finds the two servants and the soldier, whom he invites inside to hear their story. The next day they journey back together.

Peter and Cornelius represent a study in contrasts. On the one hand we have Peter feeling uncomfortable and preoccupied with his own agenda. It is difficult for us today to appreciate Simon Peter's discomfort and agitation on entering the home of a non-Jew. Fear of ceremonial defilement was stronger than a modern person's concern over exposure to infection in a room full of people suffering from contagious diseases. His opening words make his position clear. Cornelius embarrasses him by falling at his feet. Although the Roman centurion was a God-fearer who attended the Jewish temple, his old beliefs lurk beneath the surface. He learned about his visitor through an angelic visitation and so believed him to be from the gods.

The uncertainty Peter felt was not simply a personal matter, for he knew that he was taking a risk and that he would have to explain his actions to the other leaders of the church in Jerusalem. He lived in a tight-knit society in which news travelled fast. As we will see in the following chapter, no sooner had the believers throughout Judea heard about the response of the Gentiles than they began to accuse him. Peter had to hurry to Jerusalem to defend what he had done, and explain that he was simply responding to instructions from the Lord delivered both to himself in the form of a vision and to Cornelius by an angel.

Now put yourself in the sandals of Cornelius. He was so excited about the impending visit that he had called together his extended family and friends – so that there was a large number of people gathered to await Peter's arrival. That took both faith and courage. One would have hoped that Peter might have reciprocated his enthusiasm. On the contrary we find Peter's response to be cautious and distant as he draws attention to the fact that he is breaking with social convention. *'You are well aware that it against our law for a Jew to associate with a Gentile or visit him. But God has shown me that I should not call any man impure or unclean. So when I was sent for, I came without raising any objection. May I ask why you sent for me?'* Such an introduction is not likely to gain friends and influence people! If I had been Cornelius I confess that I would have been feeling a bit put out after going to all the trouble and being humiliated in front of the people I had invited. Surely Peter already knew why he had been sent for?

Even today followers of Jesus are usually more comfortable talking to each other than they are to those outside their circle. The longer they have been in the Christian sub-culture the wider became the communication gap, which then becomes blocked by a wall of prejudice. The gospel is about breaking down walls not building them and about bringing divided peoples together.

Cornelius repeats his story about how an angel had appeared to him while he was praying, telling him to send to Joppa for an individual called Simon. This was one up on Peter's story who received his revelation while he was sleeping! Cornelius lets Simon Peter know that he responded immediately, and thanks him for making the journey. He reassures his visitor that he can get straight to whatever it is he has come to tell them. *'Now we are all here in the presence of God to listen to everything the Lord has commanded you to tell us.'* Sometimes God opens up opportunities that take us by surprise, when we encounter people who are far more ready to listen and eager to ask questions than we would ever have anticipated. Their eagerness shames our reticence.

Hearing these welcoming words, Peter begins to relax and launches into his message. *'I now realise how true it is that God does not show favouritism but accepts men from every nation who fear him and do what is right.'* In other words, he recognized that these people were responding as best they could at their level of understanding.

Confess any prejudice you harbour. Ask for God's help to see everyone with the eyes of Christ and to show them his love.

He begins by assuming that his audience is familiar with the message that God sent to his people concerning peace through Jesus Christ who is Lord of all. He takes it for granted that they know about the life and ministry of Jesus, and how he was empowered by the Holy Spirit.

Considering his audience it is unlikely that they knew as much as Peter thought they did. Once again, he provides a cautionary lesson against taking too much for granted. With the current level of biblical illiteracy in Western culture, the only safe assumption to make in most contexts is that people know nothing until we have evidence to the contrary. Peter concludes his message by assuring his hearers of what he and the other close followers of Jesus have witnessed concerning his death and resurrection. As the prophets foretold, sins are forgiven through his name.

At this crucial stage of his message the Holy Spirit intervenes. His non-Jewish audience experiences the same supernatural phenomenon of speaking in tongues as had the disciples on the day of Pentecost. This is a powerful lesson to Peter and to the church that the Holy Spirit is a free agent and not controlled by the church. Likewise, in sharing the good news today, we need to be prepared for what God does through his Spirit, which we cannot predict, determine or control.

In New Testament times the communication barrier was between Jew and Gentile. Today that same barrier exists, only after nearly 2,000 years of prejudice and outbreaks of hatred, that barrier is even higher and stronger. The difference now is not how Jewish believers in Jesus can communicate the message to non-Jews, as much as how non-Jewish followers of Christ can speak meaningfully and graciously with Jewish people.

### Speaking the same language?
I don't speak the same language as you.
We don't sing from the same hymn sheet.
I don't like the things you do, your cultural expressions.
I'm sure you don't really like mine.
As long as we're clear.

I prefer to stick with my own kind,
knowing where I stand within the purity
of believers. Comfortable that no one will swear
or smoke or point my nose out of joint with a
challenge to all my beliefs and presuppositions.

I prefer to stick with my own kind,
as I said; but God, it seems, would rather I
didn't. Ouch. It's lucky that it's his love
that courses through our veins, now,
driving us from the safety of our culture.

There's a strange kind of unity
in difference. In the discomfort of
knowing that God loves you as much
as he loves me. And in the comfort of
knowing that love transcends the great divide.

For me, as much for you, that really is
Good News.

# You and your household

Acts 16:11–40

> 'Lydia was baptised along with other members of her household ... Immediately the jailer and all his family were baptised.'

Philippi presented a formidable challenge. How was Paul and his small team of helpers to begin to invite people to follow Christ and form communities of believers in a large city, where tens of thousands of people were crammed together, most living in just one-room apartments? Furthermore, how was he to penetrate a population made up of diverse peoples drawn from a large area, with a significant number of army veterans, and two-thirds of the total consisting of slaves who had no freedom to make life-changing decisions?

In addition, the missionary team had no resources to buy property from which to operate, and they realized from the outset that their stay in Philippi would be short-lived – Paul was determined not to get bogged down in one location, but to move on as soon as the church had been established in the city. He was what today we call a 'catalytic church planter', which means that he did not stay to pastor the churches he founded, but handed that role on to local leadership. A formidable challenge indeed!

In our day, churches must find new ways to establish their presence in neglected sectors of the city. The story of Paul's outreach into Philippi challenges us to think not about buildings, but people. The priority is to build a church before you build a church building, and the latter does not always follow from the former. It is by no means essential for communities of believers to build or buy their own premises. The early church managed to thrive without constructing churches for the first 150 years of its existence.

In the account of Paul's journeys in Acts he proclaimed the gospel, dialogued with his listeners, and established communities of believers. And the focus is always on people, never buildings or programmes. In Philippi the gospel gained a foothold through two very different individuals, but each was significant in that they opened up different social networks.

### Lydia the business-woman

Philippi did not have a large enough Jewish population to form a synagogue, so they held their prayer service by the local river, which provided water for their ceremonial ablutions. Paul headed there so that he could begin with his own people, as was his custom, for he believed strongly that the gospel was for the Jews first because they were God's special people.

Among the small group of Jewish workers there was at least one non-Jewish 'God-fearer', a business-woman from Thyatira, located in the Roman Province of Asia, now Western Turkey – a city renowned for its expensive purple cloth. Her clientele were among the most prosperous people in town. She did not operate her business alone, but would have a considerable 'household' to manage her affairs, import her cloth and run her home. In a culture that typically demeaned women, Lydia had broken into the male domain. She, like many other women in Roman society, was attracted to the Jewish religion because of its high moral tone and respect for her gender.

Among the group that met on the day of Paul's visit, it was Lydia whose heart God had prepared. She listened intently and the Lord opened her heart in response to Paul's teaching about who Christ was and what he came to achieve. Her response of faith was sealed in her baptism, which identified her with Christ and with his body of believers here on earth. Baptism was performed immediately because she was the first to believe and Paul would soon be moving on. But notice that she was not baptized alone, but along with other members of her household. From day one she was part of a community of faith, and she offered hospitality to Paul, which no doubt provided further opportunity for teaching. The account makes no mention of her husband, so we may assume that she was either unmarried, widowed or that her husband handled the Thyatira side of the business. What is clear is that she was an independent-minded and resourceful woman, who took the initiative to become the first Christian household in the city.

### The unnamed jailer

The second individual is someone who was not part of Paul's evangelistic strategy! Paul came into contact with the Philippian jailer as a result of having to deal with an annoying situation. His subsequent visits to the riverside prayer meeting were being constantly interrupted by the outcries of a demon-possessed slave girl. The demons, speaking through her, were claiming authority by identifying the missionaries as *'servants of the Most High God'* who had come to tell sinners how to be saved. Paul, in sheer exasperation, commands the demons to come out of her so that he can continue without further distractions. We are not told whether her deliverance resulted in her conversion. But we do know that it raised the ire of her masters, who suddenly found that they had lost their valuable source of income, for the spirits enabled her to tell fortunes with an authority that impressed a superstitious population.

They retaliated by grabbing Paul and Silas and dragging them before the authorities with the backing of a supporting mob. After a severe public beating with wooden paddles, they were thrown into prison. It is there where Paul meets his second key person – who was destined to become the leader of the next household of believers in the city. Notice that Paul and Silas, despite their unlawful treatment as Roman citizens, their painful beating, the chafing of leg-irons and the filth of a crowded maximum-security cell are still able to pray and sing far into the night.

Sometimes, it requires a spectacular or supernatural intervention to gain the attention of a life-hardened individual. In the case of the jailer, his conversion was precipitated by an earth-shaking experience. Earthquakes always come suddenly, and at any time of day or night. This one was so severe that the very foundations of the jail were shaken so that walls cracked and crumbled, bolts holding the shackles were loosened and doors sprang open. In panic people ran from the falling buildings and the prisoners saw an opportunity to escape. The jailer knew that his Roman masters would hold him personally accountable for the loss of any prisoners, and that his punishment would be a lingering death. Suicide was a preferable alternative, and an honourable way out. But, with his sword poised, Paul intervenes, reassuring the jailer that no prisoner has been lost. They are all inside.

The jailer's response suggests that he had overhead the prayers and worship of Paul and Silas. Without doubt they had also taken the opportunity to witness and preach to their captive audience. So the jailer in relief and gratitude asks the all-important question: *'What must I do to be saved?'* Paul's response is both predictable and unexpected. We would expect him to say, *'Believe on the Lord Jesus Christ,'* but he does not end there. He also includes his entire household. Earthquakes can cause sudden receptivity among people whose lives have been spared. A natural calamity can create a spiritual opportunity.

As with Lydia, we notice the emphasis on hospitality as the jailer opens his home to his captives, washes their wounds (caused by their beating and perhaps by the earthquake) and shares a meal with them. The jailer and his entire household are baptized. I wonder how long it was before the two households got together, and how many other households joined them in the coming months and years as the gospel spread throughout the city.

In a Roman city the household was one of the primary units of urban society. It consisted not only of the immediate family and nearby relatives, but also included the trusted friends of the family (*amici*) and those who regularly did business with them (*clientela*). In contemporary society we also have

Identify your 'household' – if you don't have a 'household of faith' resolve to join or form one.

our network of relationships and contacts among whom the gospel can spread.

### Freedom from captivity

I know it's not the same for everyone,
but I have to tell you:
the start of my journey was seismic –
it's the only word for it.
In the middle of the night
the ground shook, and in a flash,
my chains fell off. I was free to go.
But such glorious freedom was captivating;
it held me entranced, bound to a love
that I had never known before,
a love that rocked my world, that unleashed a force
unparalleled in my history.

Free to go, but free, too, to stay
Free to go, but free to serve.
Free to go, but free to obey.
Free to go, but free, now, to love.
Free to go, but free to remain in the house of God

and begin a different kind of sentence;
filled with words of liberation, joy and salvation.

I was shaken, I was stirred, I was quaking,
but I was truly freed, on the night
the earth moved for me.

# day 30

# An example to all

1 Thessalonians 1

'In the short time since you Thessalonians
turned to God you have became an example
to all the believers in Macedonia and
Achaia — your faith has become known
everywhere.'*

The witness of the first-century Christians resulted not only in
increasing numbers of individuals following Jesus but also in a
network of communities of believers spreading around the Mediterranean world. The churches that Paul established reproduced like
rabbits. Most churches in the Western world today are less reproduc-
tive than giant pandas! In this final day of our thirty days of reflection
we take a look at a model church planted by Paul and his team in
Thessalonica to explore what made them so spiritually fertile.

First, we note that the young church followed the example of
Paul in reflecting his eagerness for the spread of the gospel. We
reproduce after our own kind. Church leaders who themselves

demonstrate little desire and urgency to share the good news of Christ outside of their own community of faith will influence their churches to become equally self-contained. Paul, in contrast, is driven by a sense of divine urgency, which is clear not only from his missionary travels recorded in Acts, but from statements he makes in his letters to the churches.

- To the Corinthians he writes, '... *thanks be to God, who always leads us in triumphal procession in Christ and through us spreads everywhere the fragrance of the knowledge of him*' (2 Corinthians 2:14).
- To the Colossians he rejoices that the gospel that had come to them in such a marvellous fashion was bearing fruit and growing in the whole world (Colossians 1:6).
- To the Christians in Rome he brings a word of encouragement that their faith is proclaimed in all the world (Romans 1:8).

His vision infected and inspired new believers in Jesus and motivated the new households of faith to spread the message and to invite others to follow in their steps.

Furthermore, these groups of believers refused to be intimidated into silence by their opponents. The church grew, as in many places around the world today, in the face of opposition. The church in Thessalonica was no exception (see Acts 17:1–10). No sooner was the church born than their Jewish opponents incited a mob to riot in the city. When they failed to locate Paul, they dragged Jason and some of the other believers before the city officials. Jason was singled out for welcoming Paul and his team into his home. They were charged with treason for calling Jesus Lord in place of Caesar. They were required by the authorities to post bond as a guarantee against causing further trouble, and that night they sent Paul and Silas out of the city under cover of darkness.

So Paul can say to them, '*You became imitators of us and of the Lord.*' A believer's commitment in following Christ inevitably leads to having to face the hostility of the world. The believers in Thessalonica also shared in the experience of Paul and his Lord in knowing the joy of the Holy Spirit in the midst of adversity.

Paul's statements are even more remarkable when we recognize that the church in Thessalonica was only a few weeks or months old when Paul wrote this letter. Yet, in a short space of time the message of the gospel had spread from them throughout the two Roman provinces of Achaia and Macedonia, which make up most of modern Greece. These Spirit-filled believers were irrepressible. The Lord's message 'rang out' from them. Their voice was as attention-getting as the sounding of a bugle, or the roar of a waterfall, or the clap of thunder. Their faith had become known everywhere.

Here we see two principles at work. The first is that an abundant spiritual harvest requires the abundant sowing of the seed of the gospel. The second is that new believers make the most effective witnesses. Why? On account of their enthusiasm, the impressive change that the gospel has brought about in their lives, and the fact that most, if not all, of their relatives, friends and acquaintances are not yet believers.

Notice the three essential steps in the progress of the gospel.
- *It came to you* (verse 5)
- *You received it* (verse 6)
- *You passed it on* (verse 8)

And we might add, they wasted no time in doing it!

In these opening paragraphs of the letter, Paul reflects on the impact that his message had had on them. He recalls how God's power had been in evidence in his preaching. He had spoken with great conviction, aware that there was a divine urgency in his message, as he saw the impact of his words on those who had gathered to hear him. Where the Holy Spirit is, communication becomes super-charged! And that power is not simply the emotion of the moment. It leads to life transformation.

For the Thessalonians it led to a profound change of allegiance. They had formerly been slaves to idols, now they had turned away from them to serve the living God with total allegiance. This was a costly step because their involvement in government, trade, recreation and social life all required that they worship the appropriate gods. But Jesus provided them with release from this spirit-haunted world over which he had triumphed by his resurrection from the dead. The believers now lived in eager anticipation of Jesus' return to earth from heaven, when he would come to judge the earth and to rescue his people.

Paul spells out the key characteristics of genuine believers. You can see who is for real by three benchmarks, he says. First is *their faith-inspired work*. They are not simply workaholics, driven by ambition or the need to prove themselves to God, their fellow believers, or their leaders. They work as those who see the invisible. They are living in anticipation of God's future kingdom. Their faith is inspired by their trust in a God who has declared his intentions to them and whom they know will not let them down. Their toil is never reduced to drudgery.

The second benchmark is their *love expressed in labour*. Their love is not simply a warm feeling, but sweaty toil. Paul is referring to the kind of sacrificial love that the Father demonstrated in sending his only Son into the world. He is referring to the kind of love that

What are the key things God has spoken to you about during these 30 days? Resolve to follow up areas where God is prompting you to change or grow.

Jesus demonstrated in laying down his life for his friends. It is a love that refuses to give up, whatever the cost. Such love constantly takes the initiative rather than waiting for someone else to step forward. It is love that demonstrates unreserved commitment and determined effort. Followers of Jesus are able to demonstrate this quality of love only because they themselves have been called to experience that love, which is now channelled through them. This is the assurance that Paul expresses concerning them, when he describes them as loved by God, and reminds them that they are chosen by him.

The third benchmark is *hope-inspired endurance*. Whenever hope is linked with the gospel it carries the meaning of rock-firm confidence rather than wistful resignation. It is a hope that is defiant and unconquerable. It is hope 'no matter what'. Faith, love and hope provide the three pillars of spiritual stability as well as the hallmark of spiritual vitality.

### New beginnings
Every new beginning is
some other new beginning's
end.

At the end of this journey, we are
setting out once more.

Challenged, preparing to go
and live up to the challenge.

'Are you receiving me?' The word of God
crackles through the atmosphere as we
tune in to a new frequency.

The world is our oyster;
and we have found a pearl of
great price.

Are you receiving me? Then pass it on!
Give it away! Go, now, and give it away.

This is no hopeless cause;
this is no senseless journey.
Use all your senses, heightened
by your response to a Creator
in whose image you have been crafted.

Taste the divine.
See the need.
Hear the call.
Catch the fragrance of the eternal.
Touch the world.

This is no senseless journey.

Jesus never promised that the road will be easy,
but we have a guide, and a travelling companion,
a Spirit of hope along the Way.

Walk with expectancy. And as you walk,
look at those around you;
some will give you support, others will look for yours.
You are not alone; we are never alone
but we travel together, to the ends of the world
and way, way beyond.

We are caught between an age that is passing,
and an age that is to come. Yet
today is the day of our salvation.

We are going on a journey. Now,
walk with expectancy, along the road
less travelled. Go well.

### Postscript

Day 30 represents the end of the beginning. For the journey of faith
lasts a lifetime and we cannot walk alone. We walk in a company
that must never close ranks, but is always urgently and respectfully
inviting others to join their number and, in so doing, enrich their
communal life.